# SUNRISES
## of County Clare, Ireland
### Mystical Moods of Ireland, Vol. VII

# SUNRISES
## of County Clare, Ireland

### Mystical Moods of Ireland, Vol. VII

James A. Truett

www.JamesTruettBooks.Com

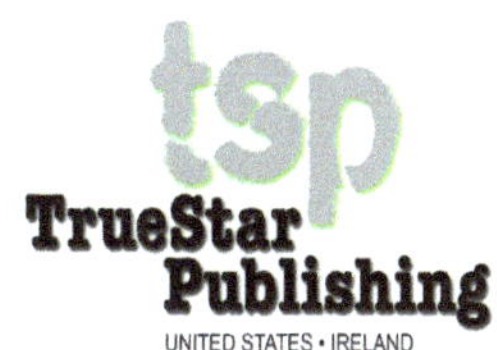

Published by TrueStar Publishing
United States • Ireland
*www.TrueStarPublishing.Com*

**Ordering Information:**
All products in the Moods of Ireland series including books, calendars, posters, cards and prints are available at special quantity discounts for bulk purchases for sales promotions, premiums, fund raising, educational, corporate or institutional use. Specially customized books, calendars, posters, cards and prints can also be created to fit specific needs. For details, please e-mail the publisher at:
specialsales@truestarpublishing.com

**PBK-ISBN-13:** 978-1-948522-13-7
**PBK-ISBN-10:** 1948522136
**HBK-ISBN-13:** 978-1-948522-12-0
**HBK-ISBN-10:** 1948522128

**First Edition:** March 2020

10 9 8 7 6 5 4 3 2 1

**COVER:** *"Spectacular Irish Sunrise over Shannon Estuary, County Clare" by James A. Truett.*

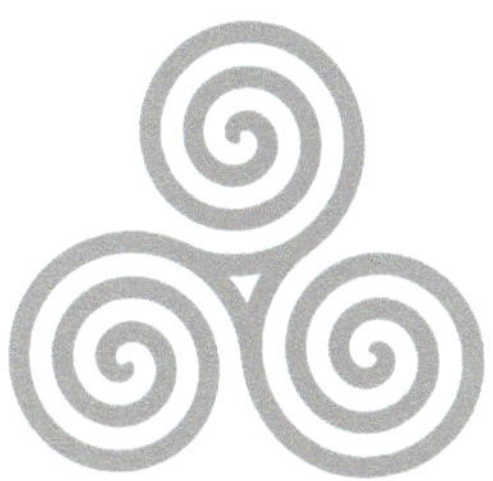

# Dedication

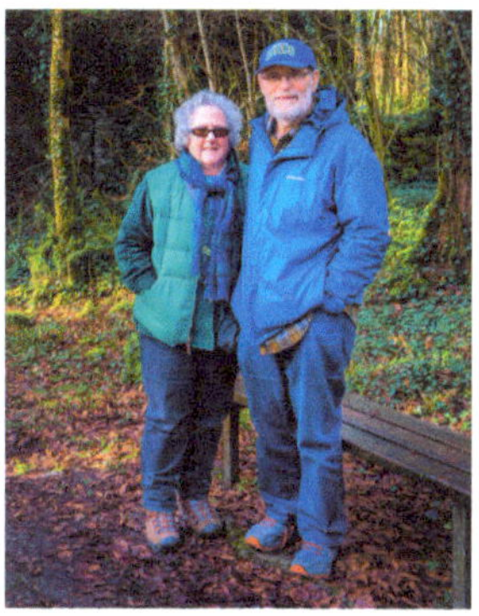

*For my friends*
**David & Elizabeth Odell**

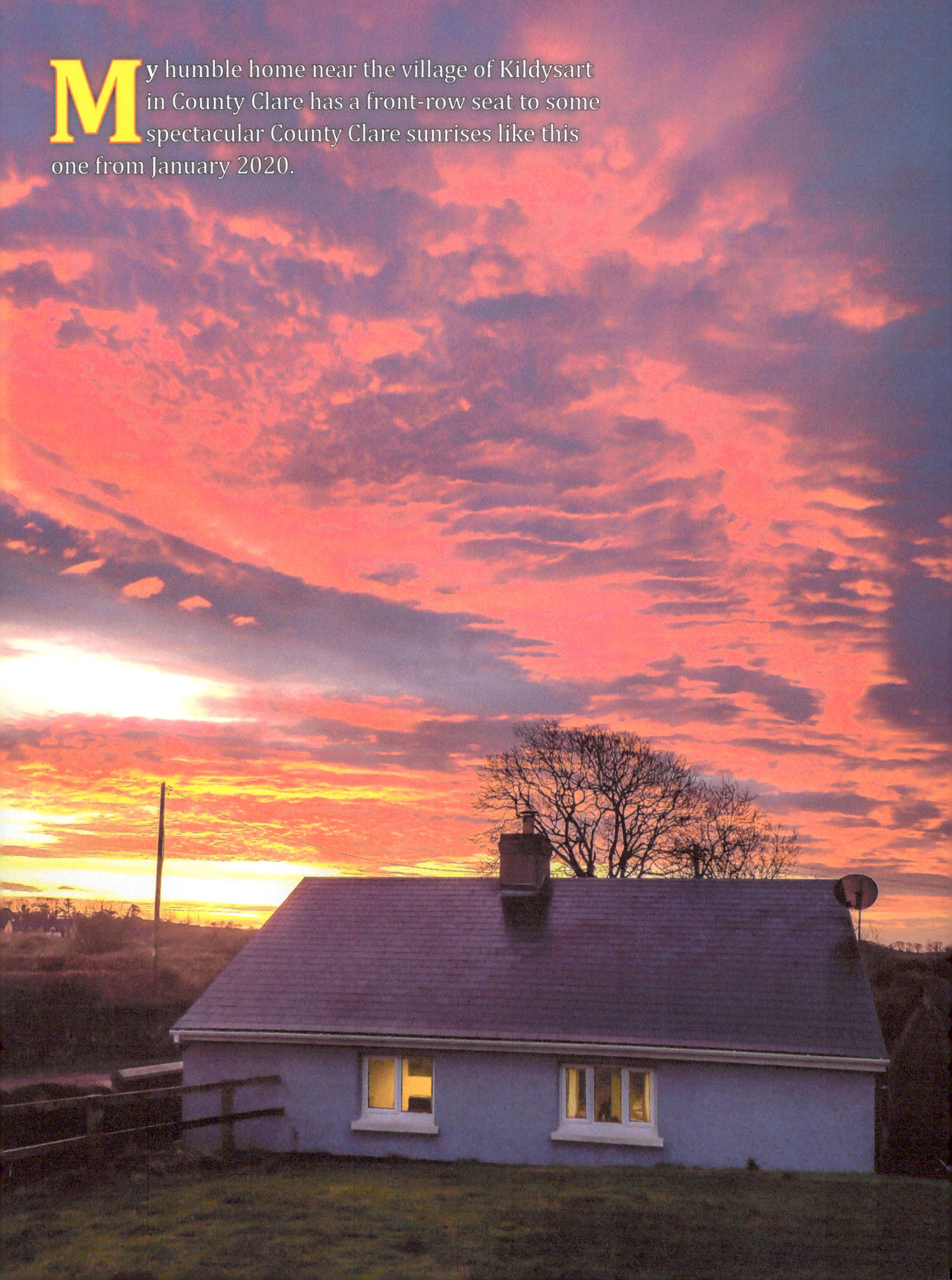


**M**y humble home near the village of Kildysart
in County Clare has a front-row seat to some
spectacular County Clare sunrises like this
one from January 2020.

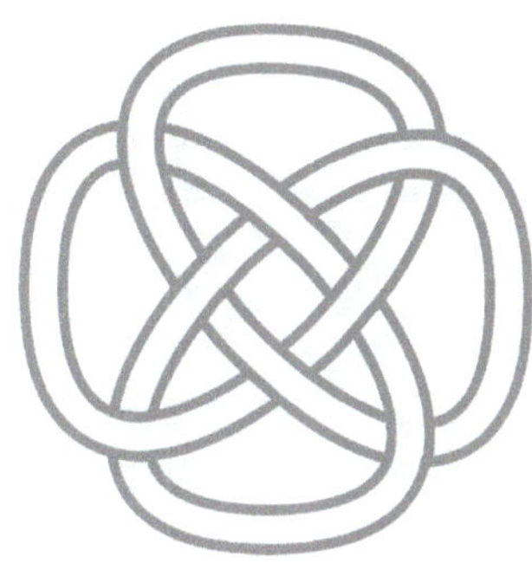

# Introduction
## *Sunrises of County Clare, Ireland*

**S**ince prehistoric times, humans have marvelled at the brilliant colours and patterns in the sky at sunrise, conjuring myths and legends in an attempt to explain these spectacular displays.

Ancient cultures worldwide created stories of deities and demons traversing the skies in a perpetual war between good and evil, darkness and light.

The Celtic culture viewed sunrises as a rebirth or reawakening — a conquering of the forces of darkness — with the spirits of nature granting the world a new day.

Mariners still read the skies for hints of winds and weather in the cloud formations and colours (Red sky in morning, sailor take warning.)

If you're like me, amazing sunrises like those I see here in County Clare are reminders to take a moment and appreciate the natural beauty that remains in our world.

No matter your religious or spiritual beliefs, my hope is that you find many moments of peace and tranquillity in the pages of this book.

Go raibh mile maith agat! *(A thousand thank yous!)*

**James A. Truett**
County Clare, Ireland

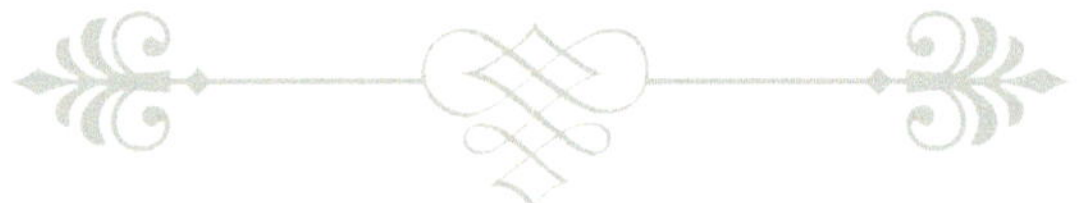

## Reflections on an Irish Country Road

**A** damp country road bordered by perpetually green meadows near the village of Kildysart reflects the brilliant colours of this December sunrise.

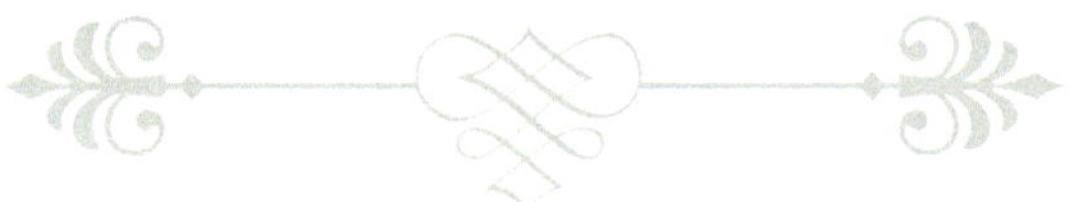

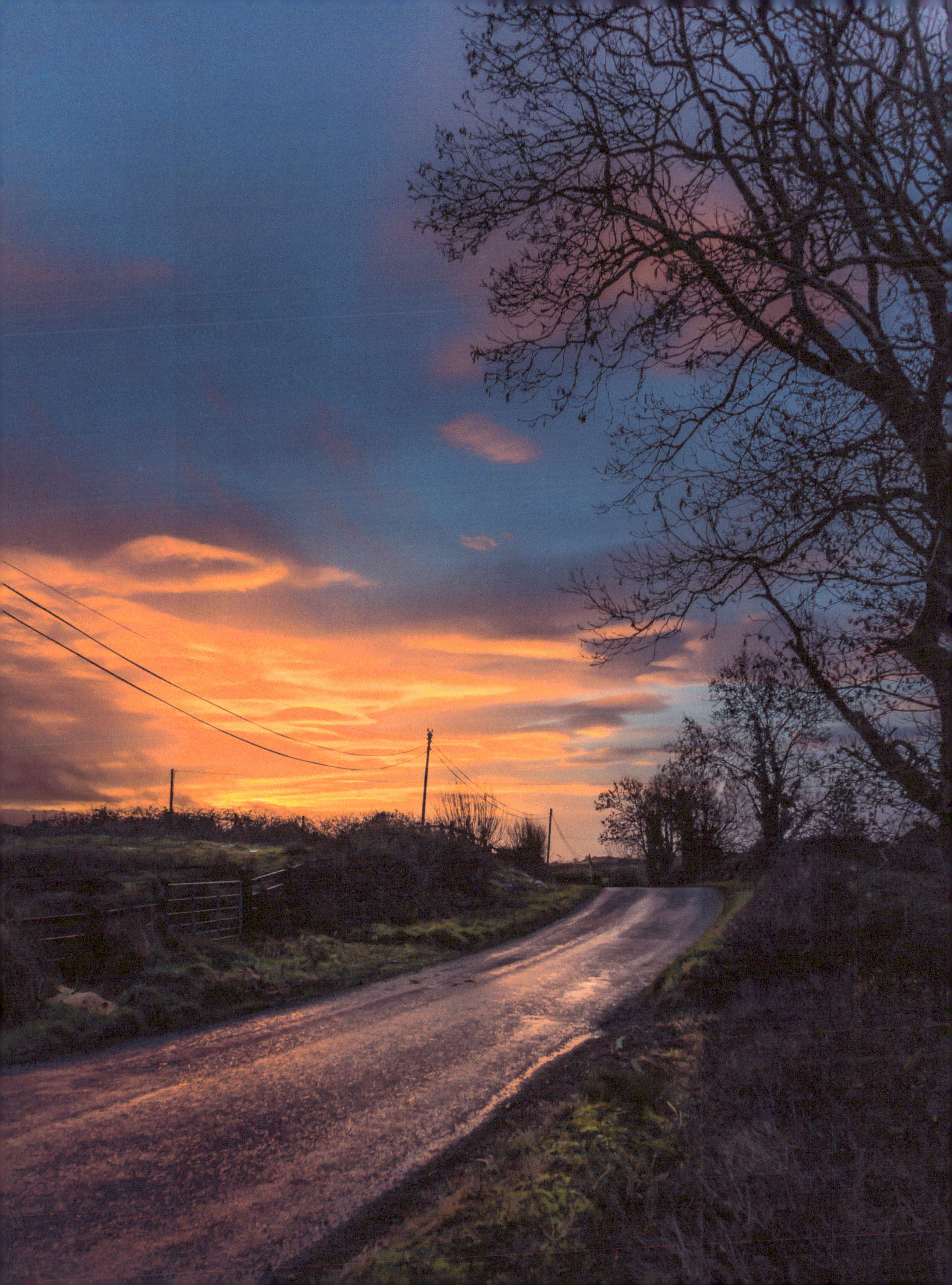

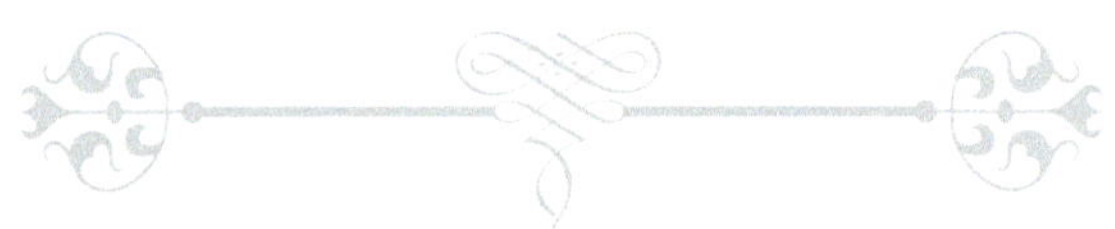

## Last Breath of Autumn

A scarlet and orange sky provides a dramatic backdrop to this tree, with its assortment of tentacles reaching for a last breath of Autumn, before settling into its Winter sleep.

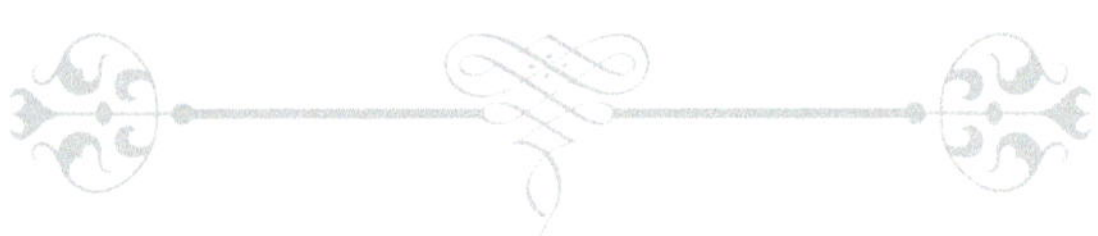

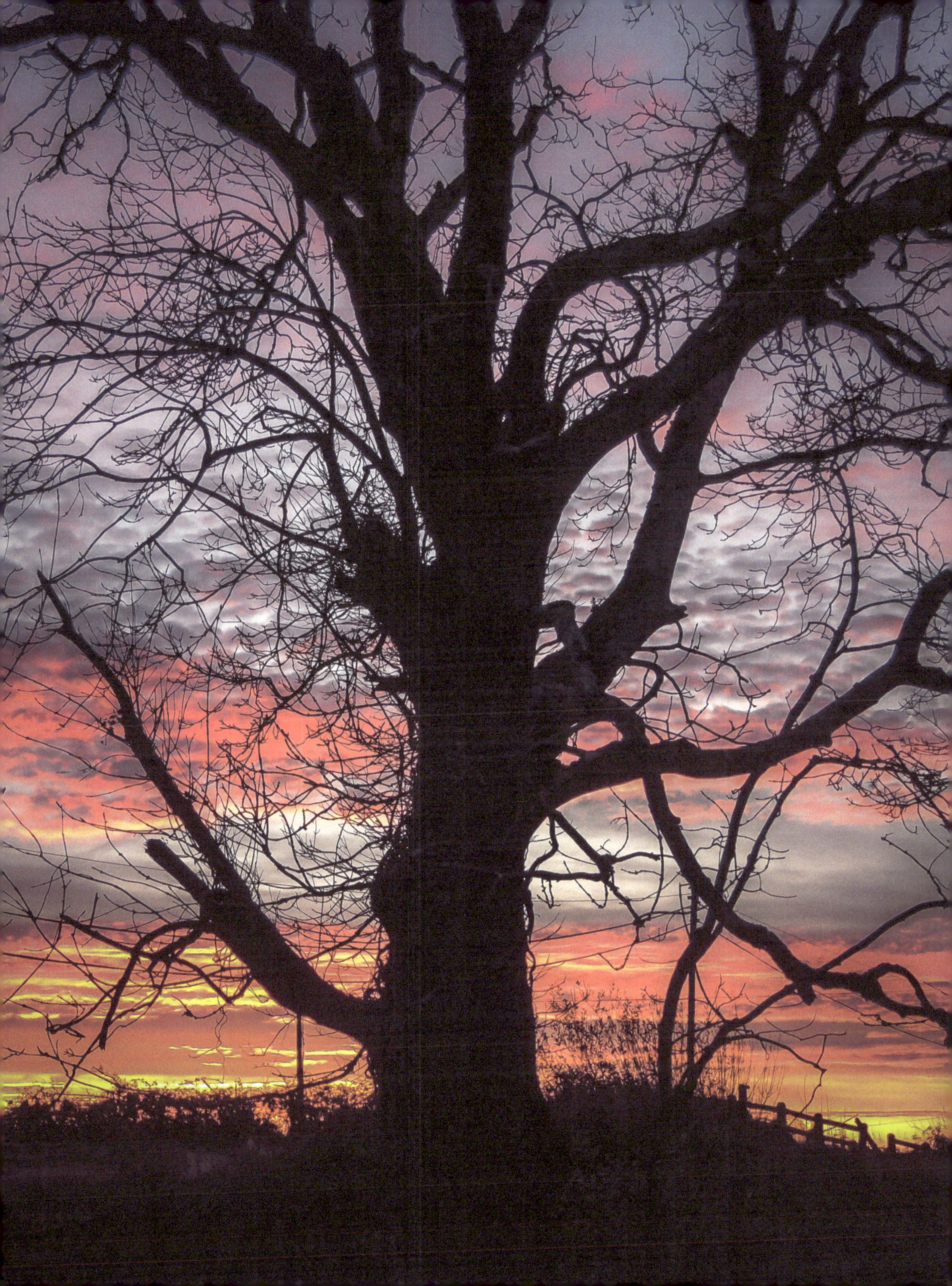

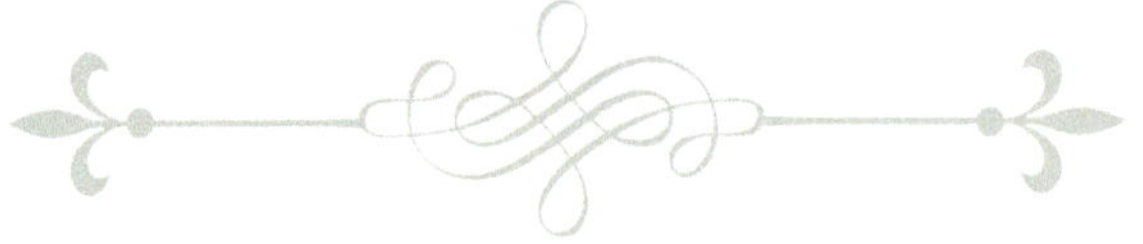

## September Sunrise over Kildysart

A September sunrise battles with diminishing jet trails to announce dawn over the village of Kildysart, along the shores of Ireland's Shannon Estuary.

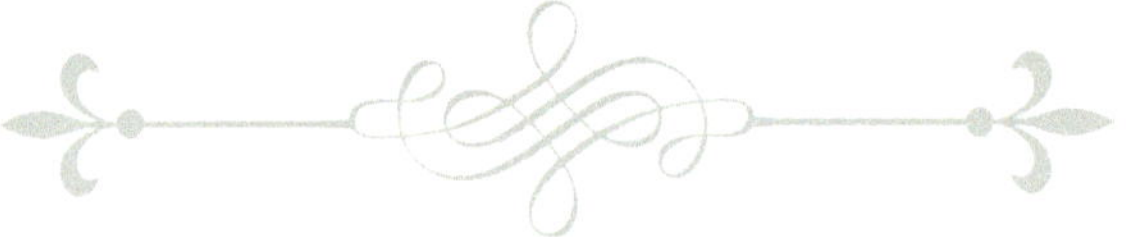

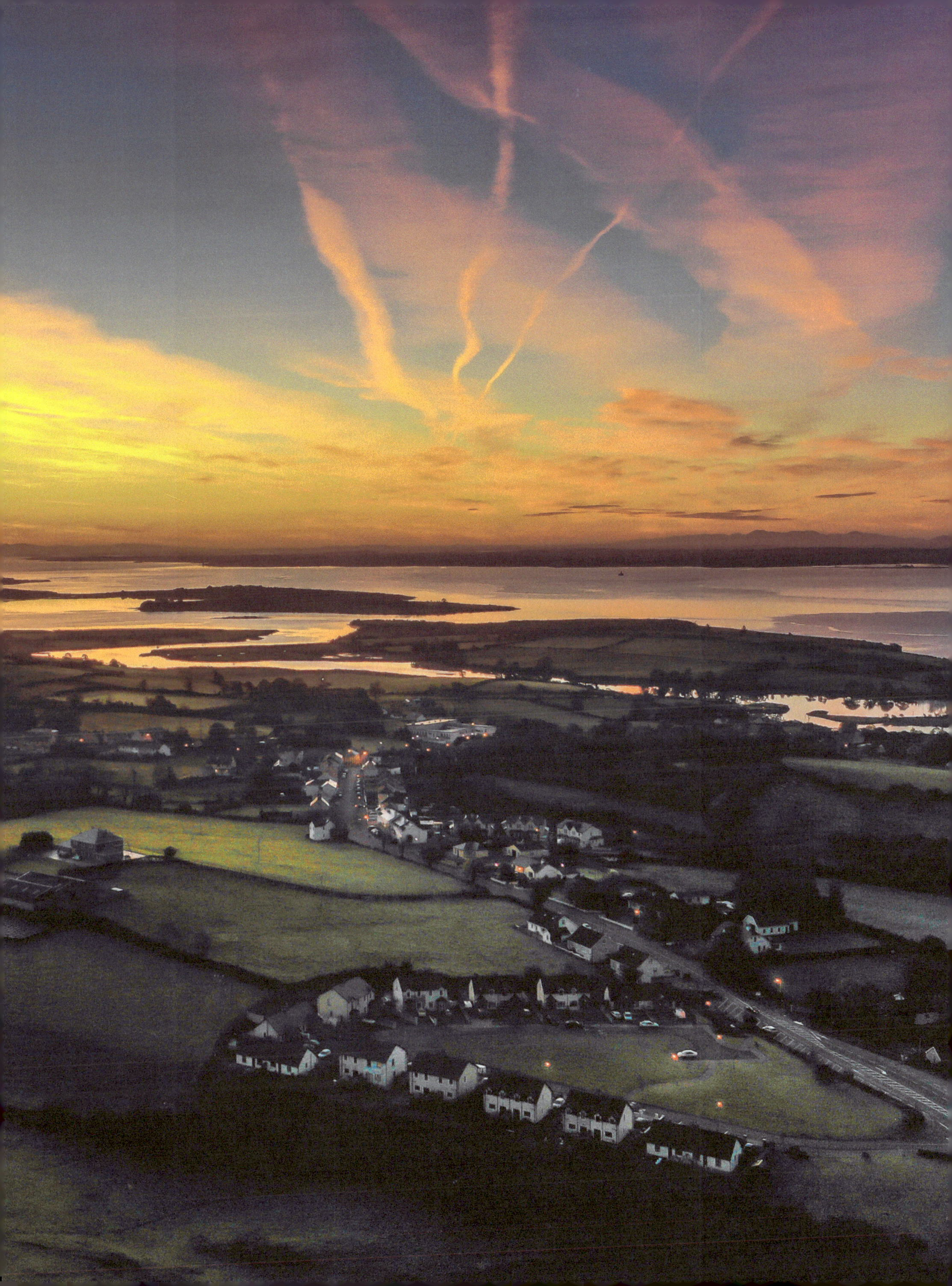

## Boiling Clouds at Sunrise

October clouds boil in the rays of the rising sun over Kildysart, now a sleepy hollow of less than 1,000 residents. The village once was home to more than 4,000 people prior to the famine years of the mid-1800s.

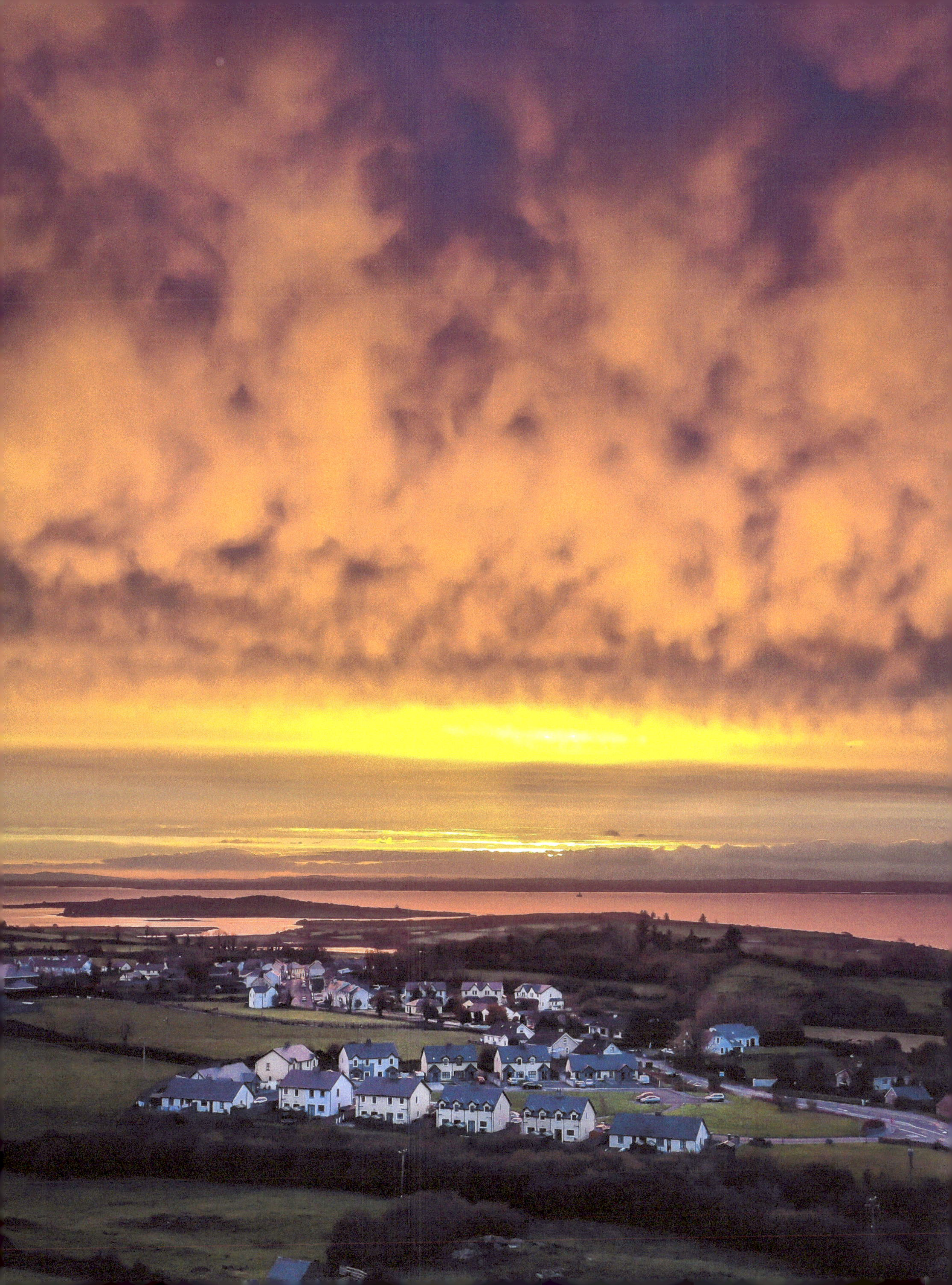

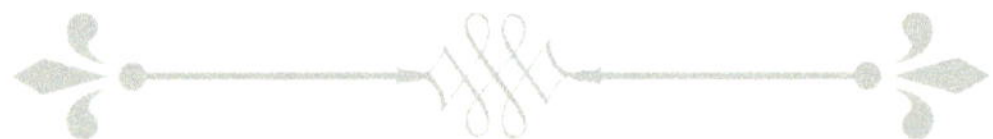

## Ballylean Lake at Sunrise

**T**his small lake surrounded by green pastures in the townland of Ballylean reflects the sun-painted sky during a May sunrise.

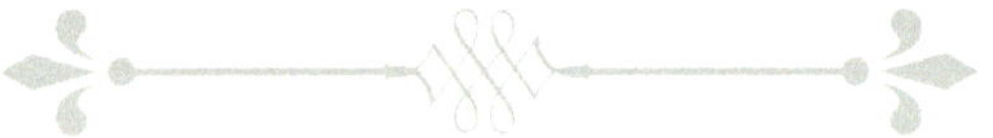

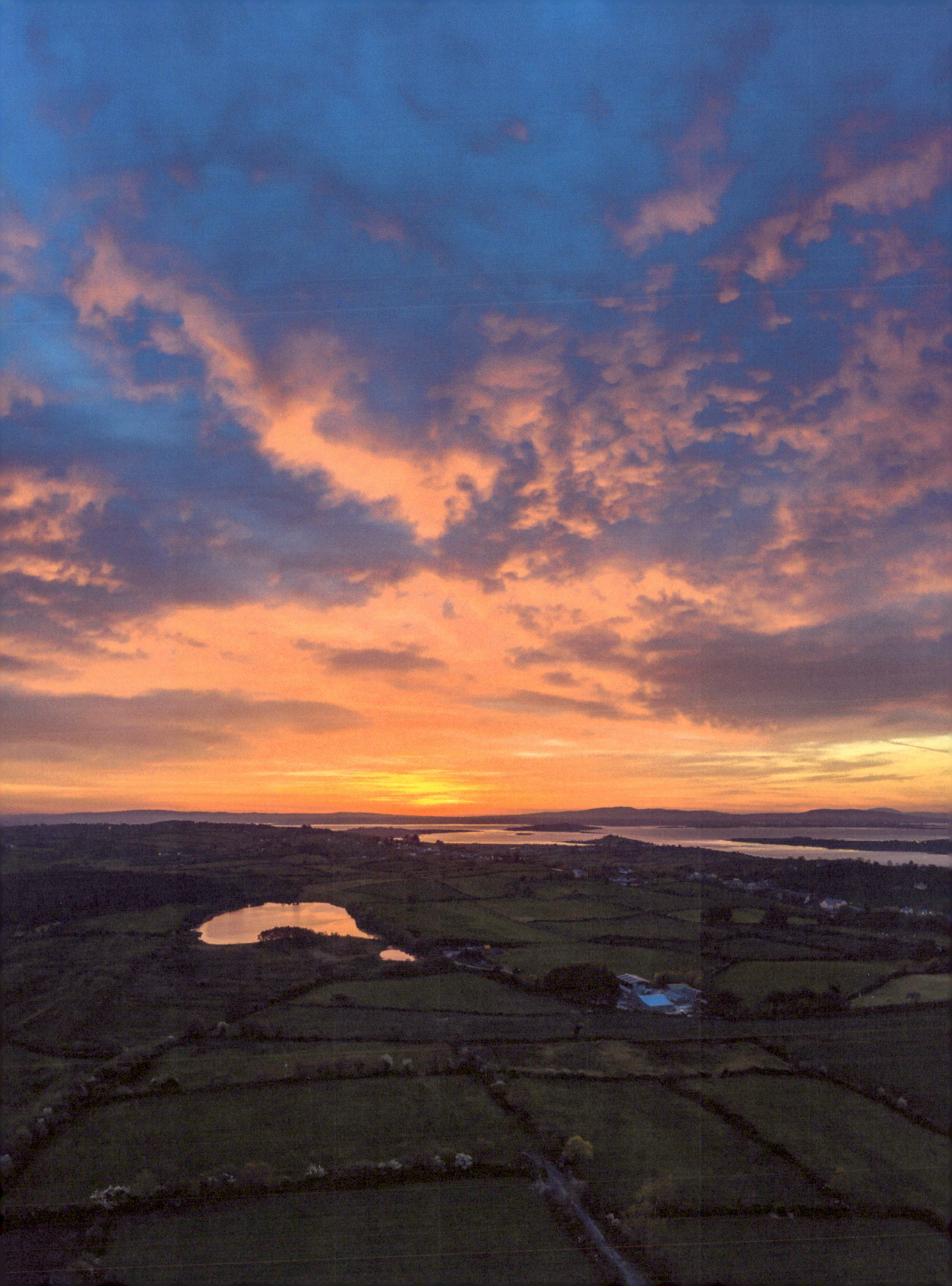

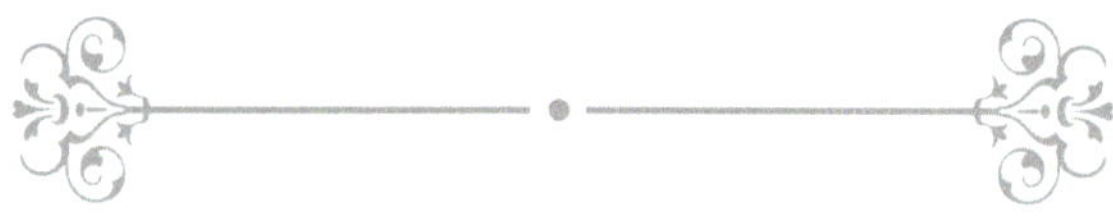

## Sunrise at Kildysart Quay

In years past, this part of the Shannon Estuary was a popular trade and supply route for County Clare and western Ireland. Kildysart was a regular stop for river freighters transporting food, livestock and building supplies.

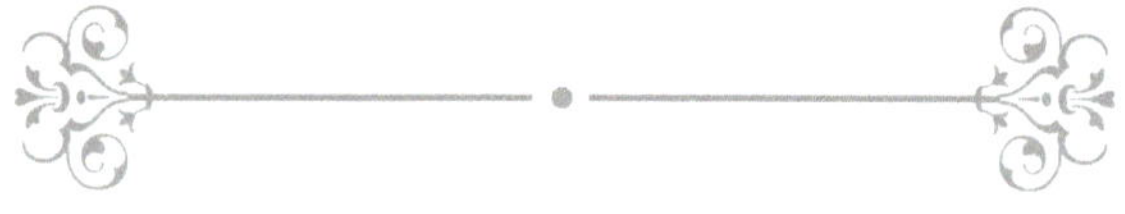

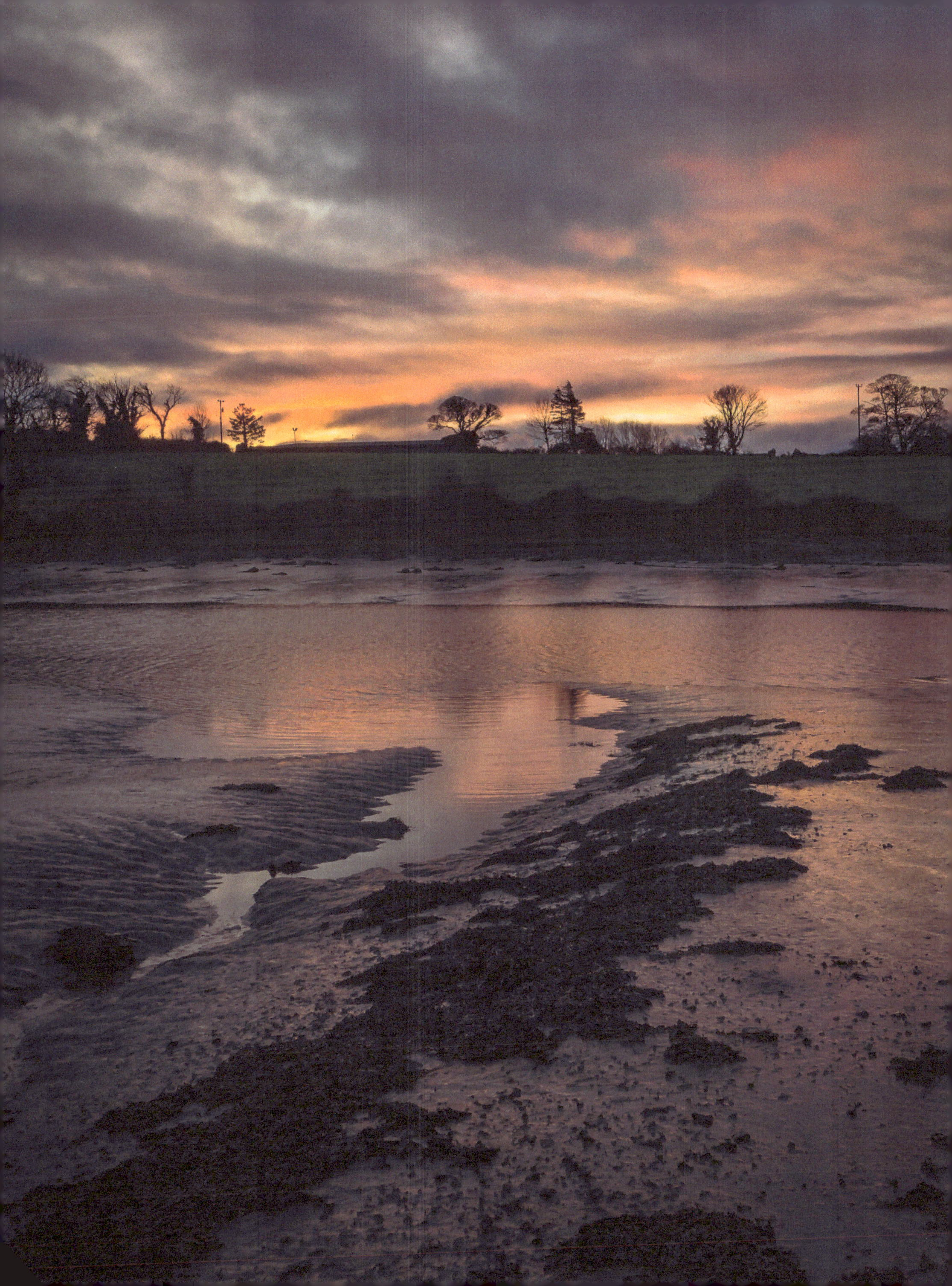

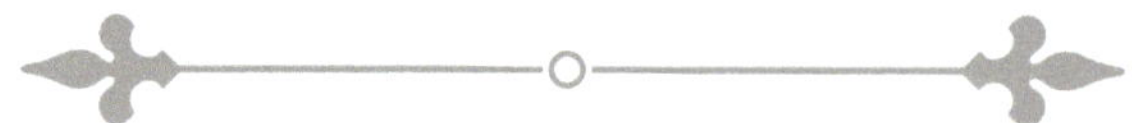

# Shannon Estuary Tidelands and Islands

**S**hannon Estuary with its many small islands was home to a significant population including monks at a 12th Century Augustinian monastery on Canons' Island and many farmers and their families on surrounding islands. Residents eventually died or moved ashore.

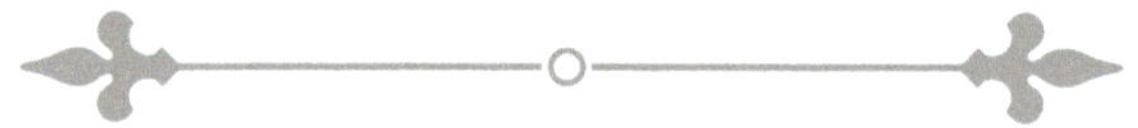

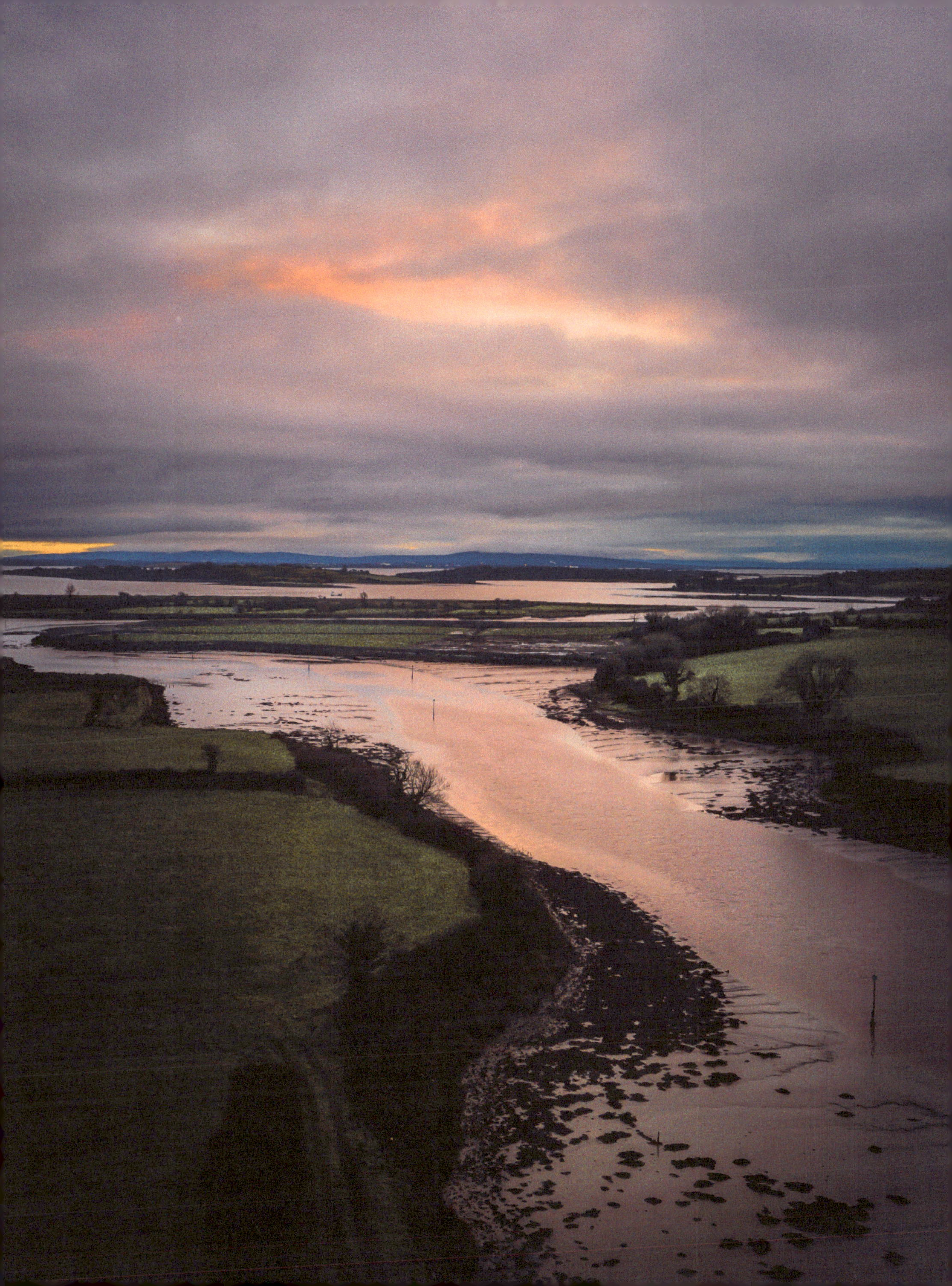

## White Horse at Sunrise from Crovraghan

A horse grazes under a September sunrise over the rolling green pastures of County Clare along the shores of the Shannon Estuary at the townland of Crovraghan.

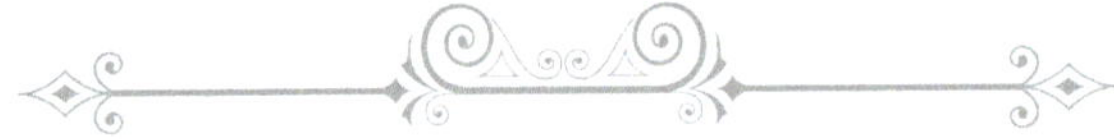

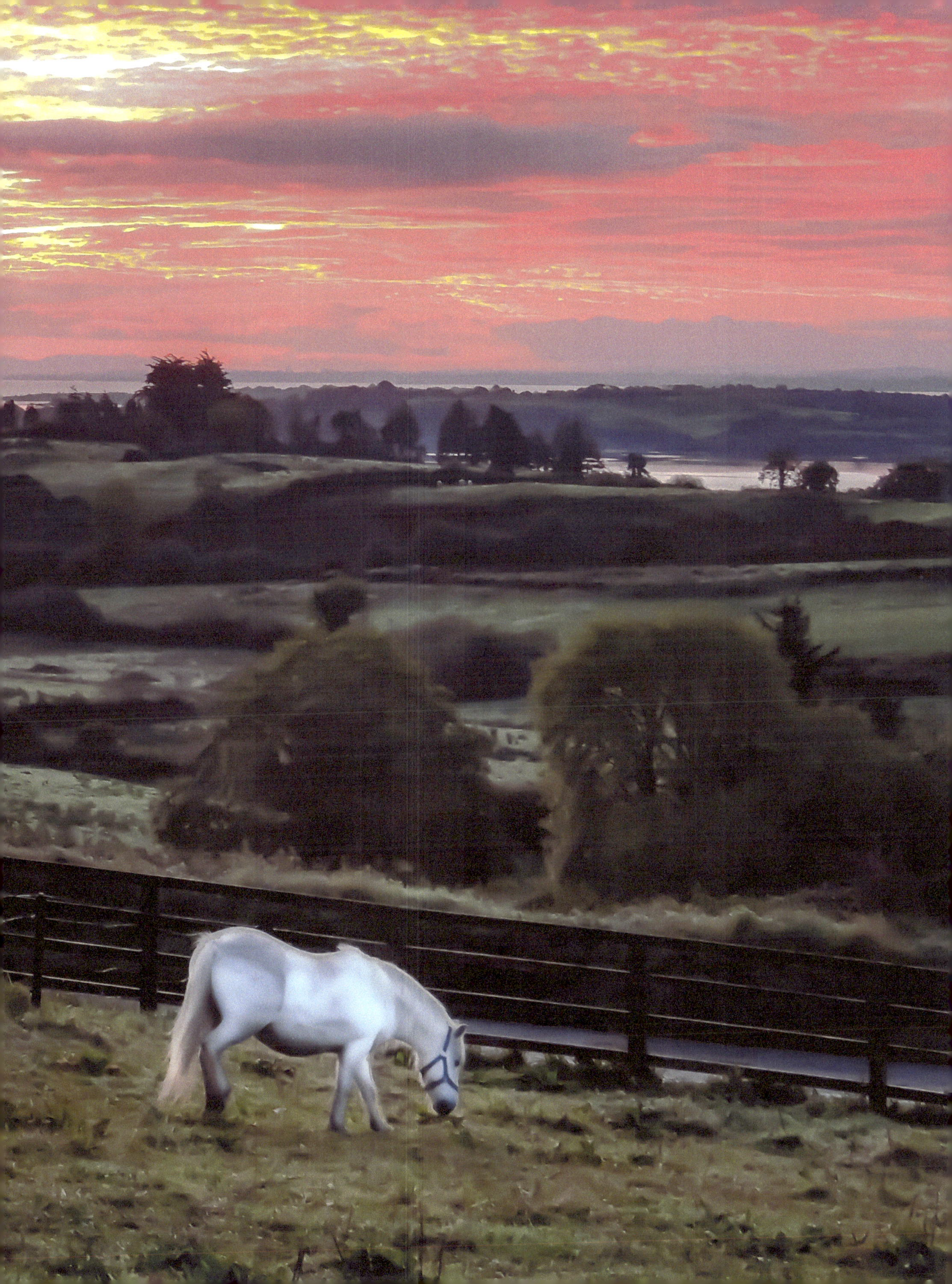

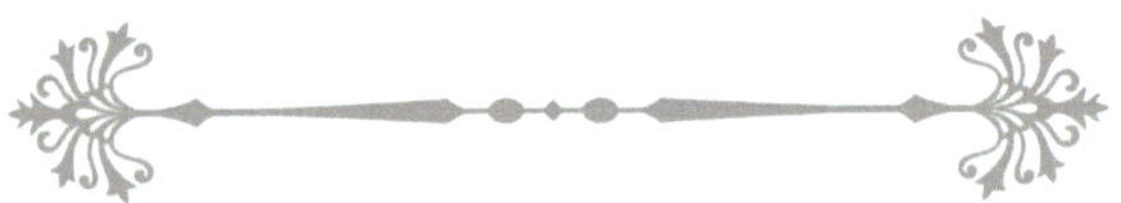

## Wispy September Sunrise

A variety of cloud formations act as the canvas for a palette of sunrise colours over the County Clare countryside.

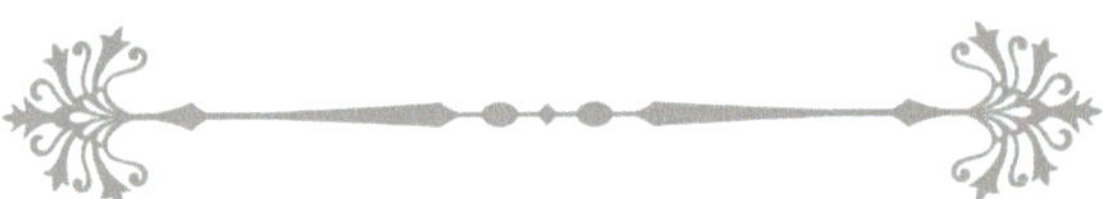

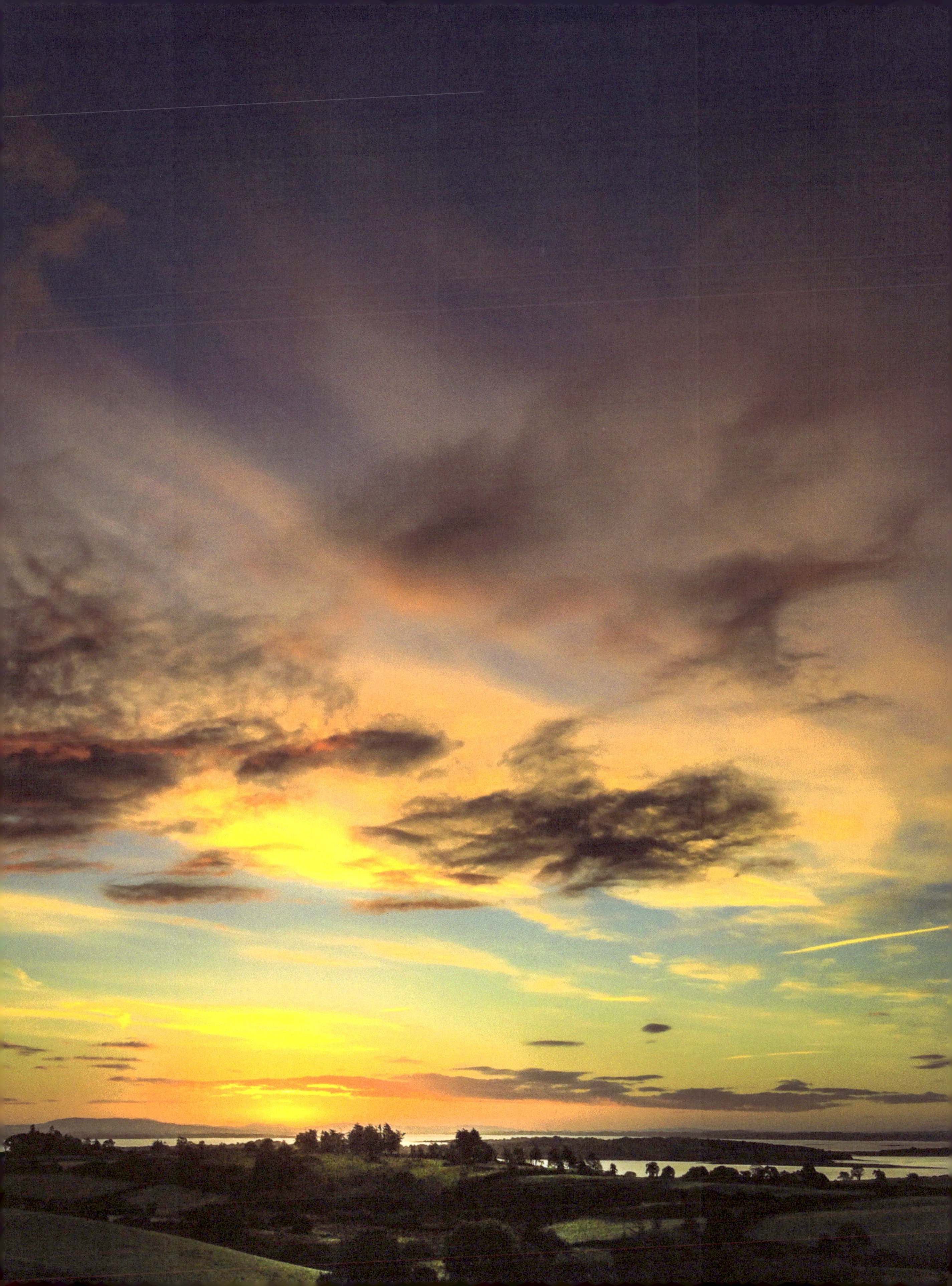

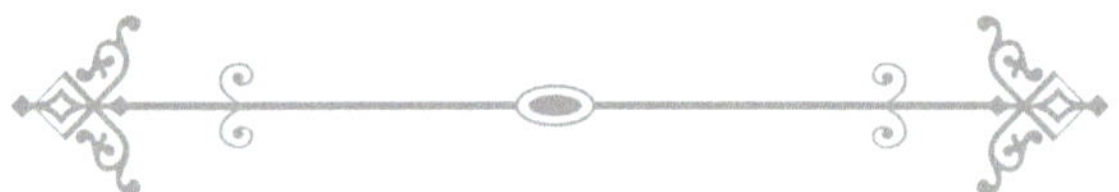

## Layered November Sunrise

**A**n early November morning presented this appearance of a layered sunrise with colours reflecting in Ireland's Shannon Estuary. In the distance are the shores of County Limerick.

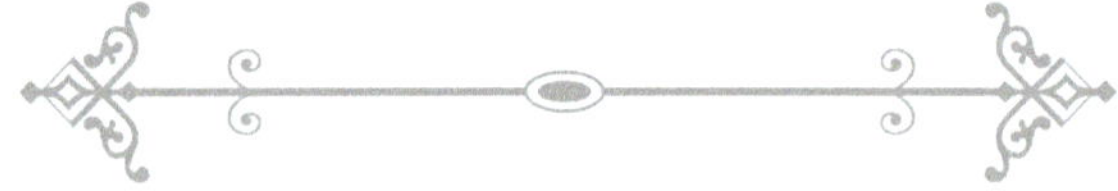

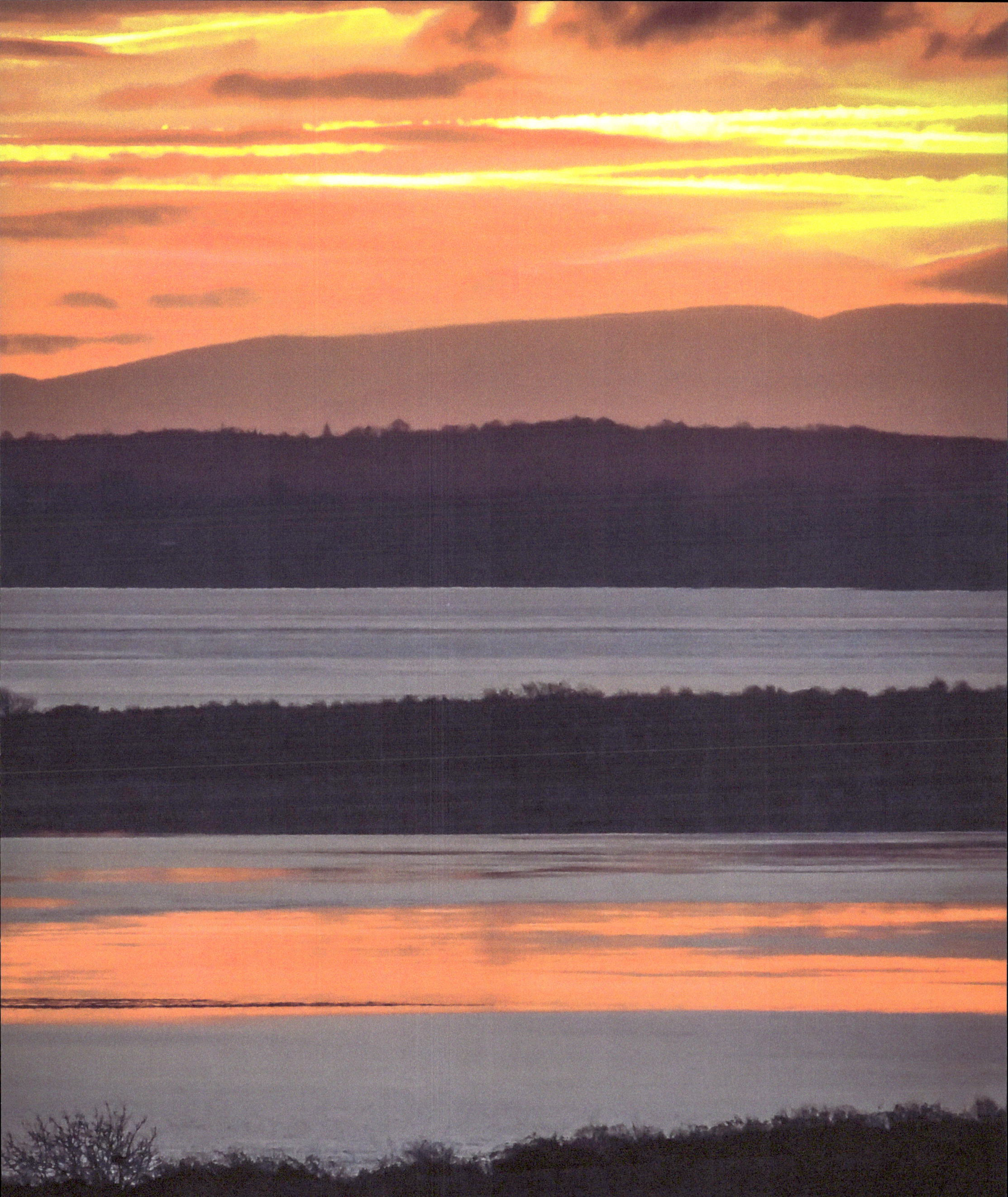

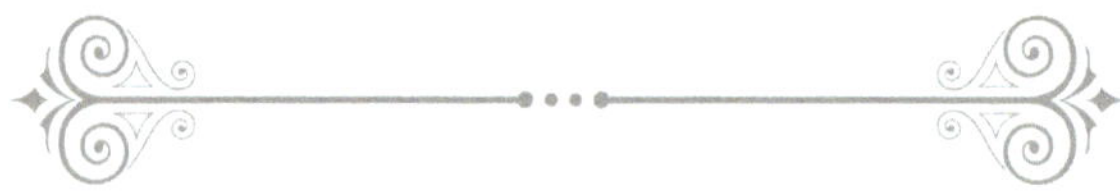

## Crimson Sunrise

**A** breathtaking November morning began with this soul-stirring crimson sky over Ireland's Shannon Estuary.

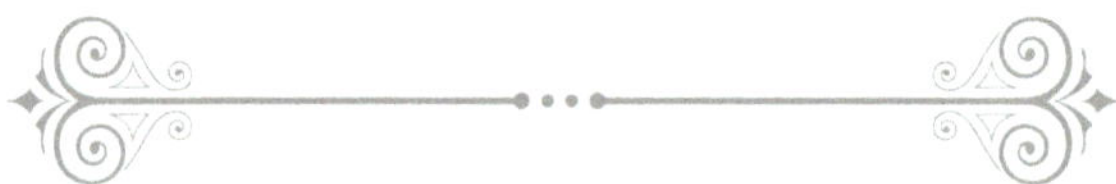

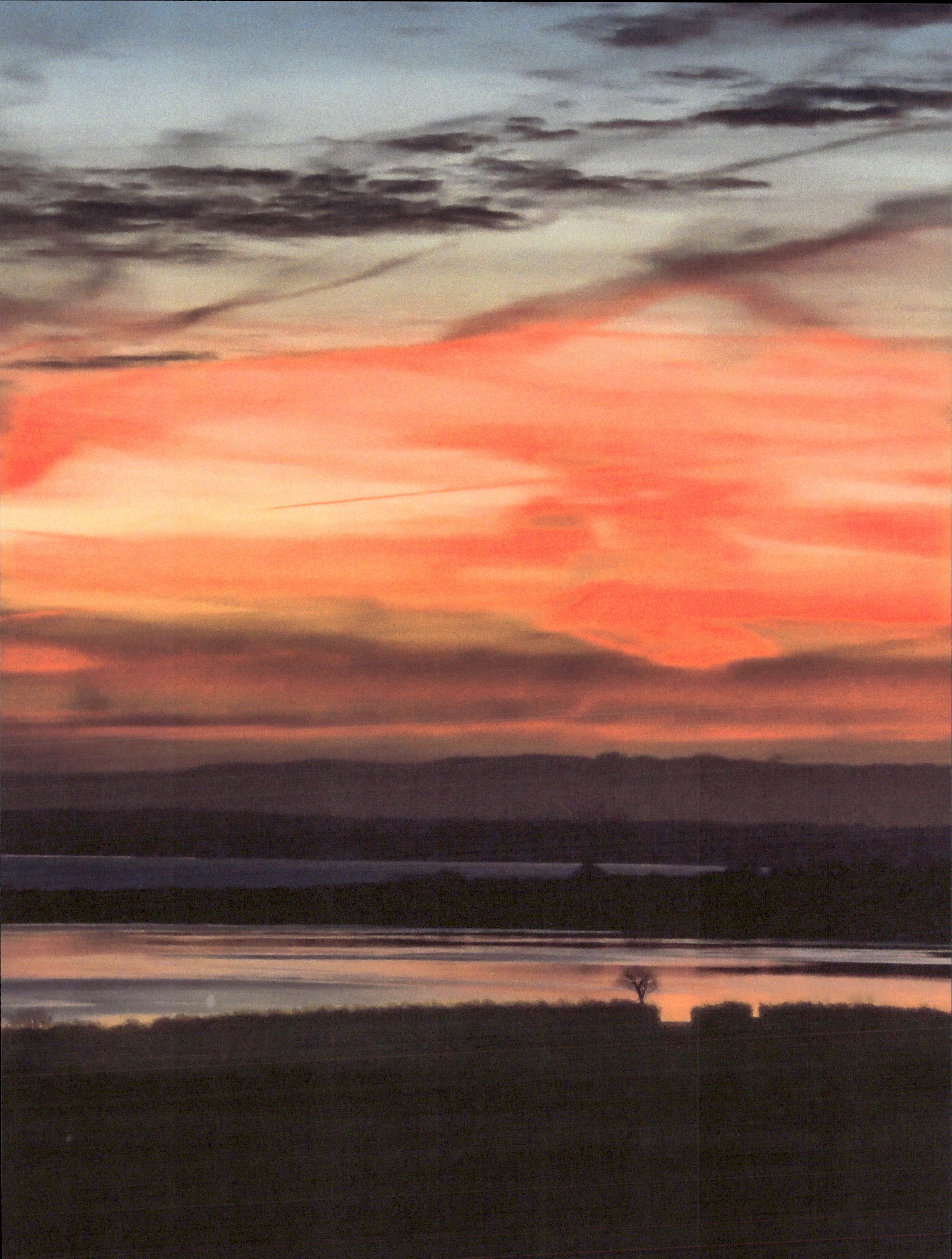

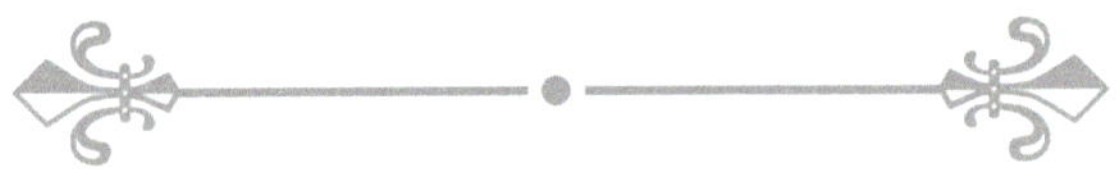

## November Sunrise Reflections

**A** brilliant sun and orange sky reflect in the ever-moving waters of the Shannon Estuary at Crovraghan. No sunrise is ever the same.

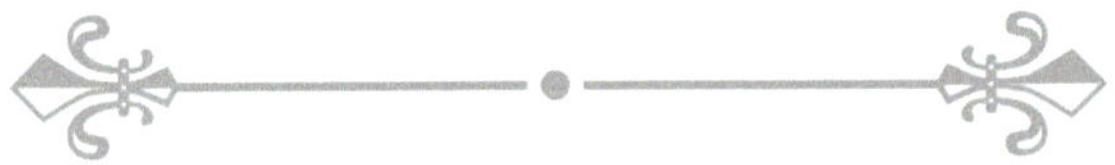

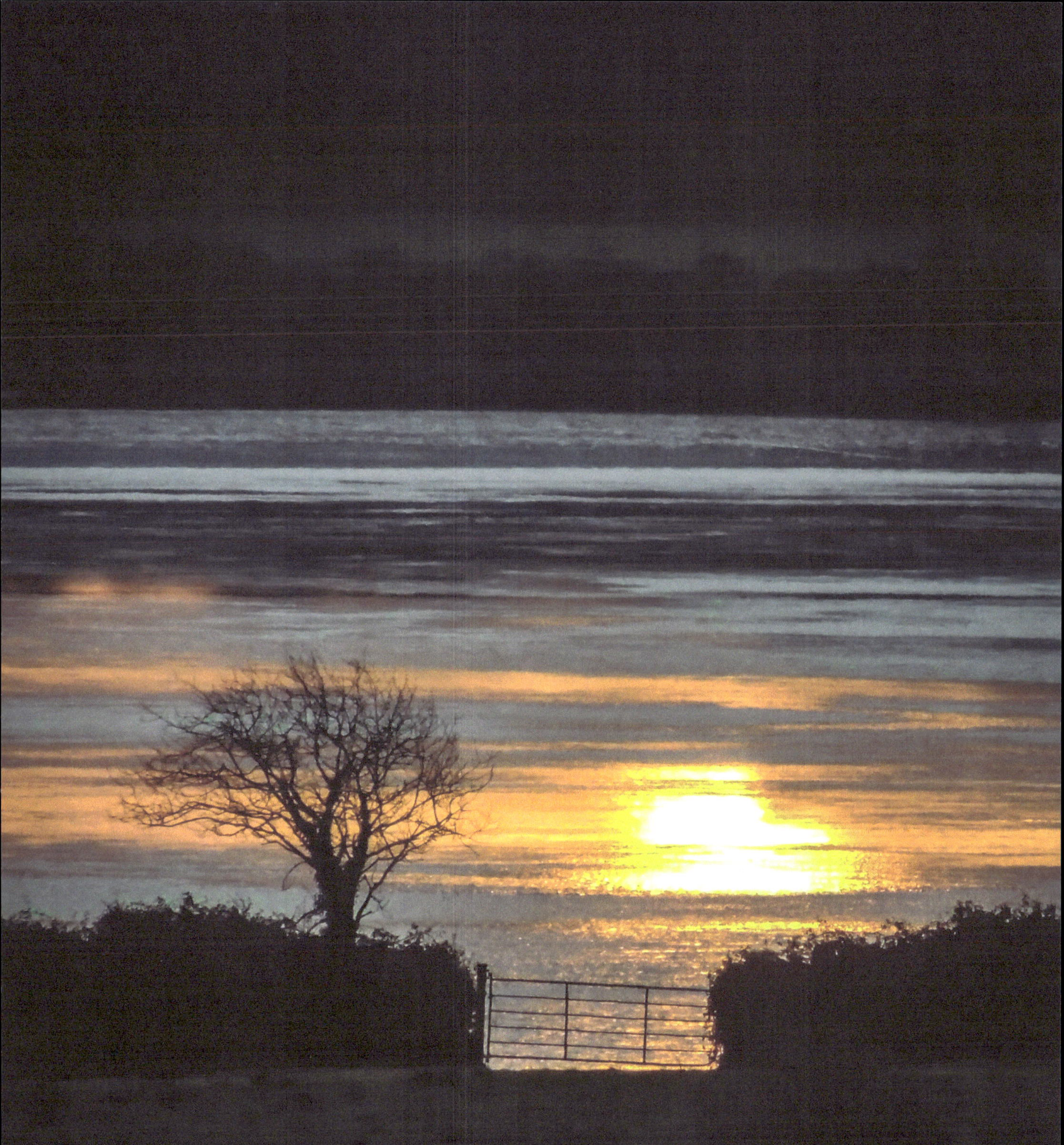

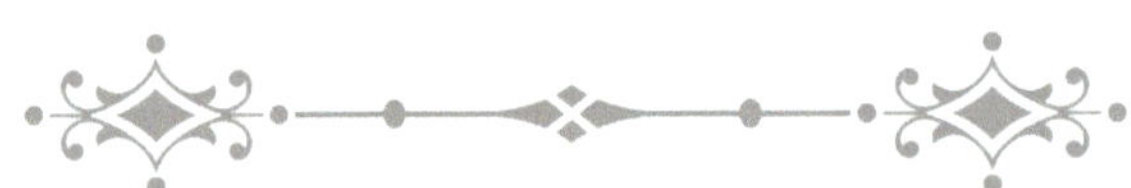

## Bursting Sun Rays

A January sky pits sunbeams against dark clouds over a Crovraghan meadow along the Shannon Estuary near the village of Kildysart.

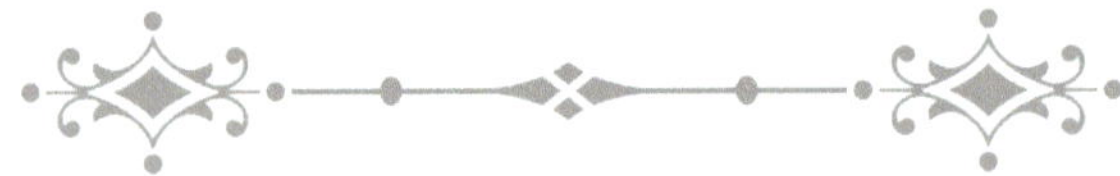

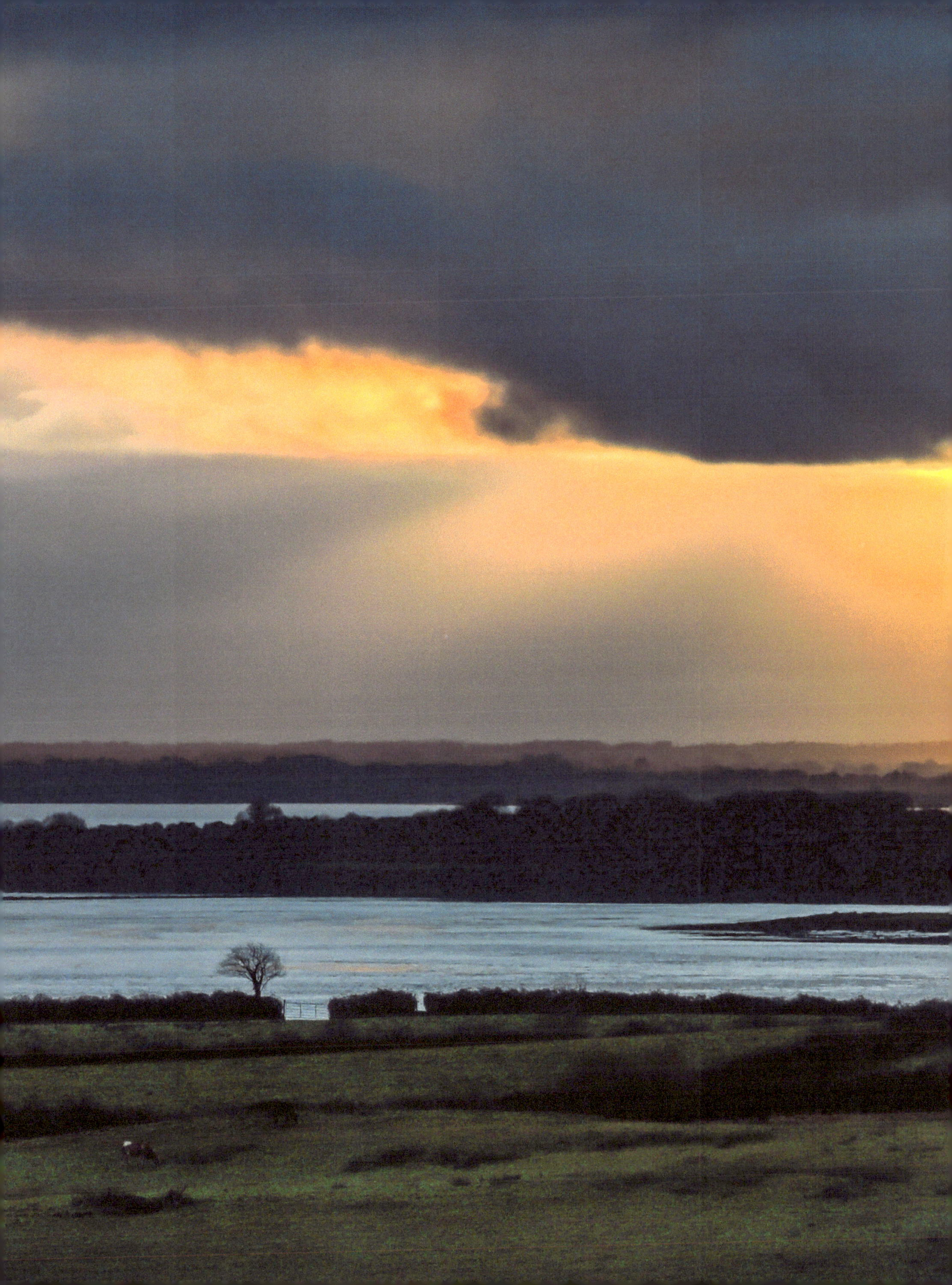

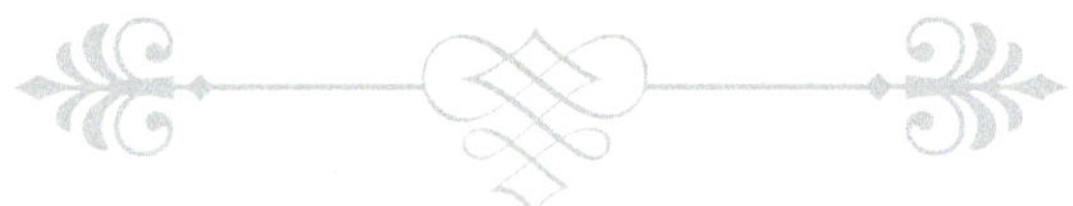

## Tangerine Sunrise

An intense tangerine sky accompanies this November sunrise over the Shannon Estuary as dark clouds fight to maintain their grip on the impending day.

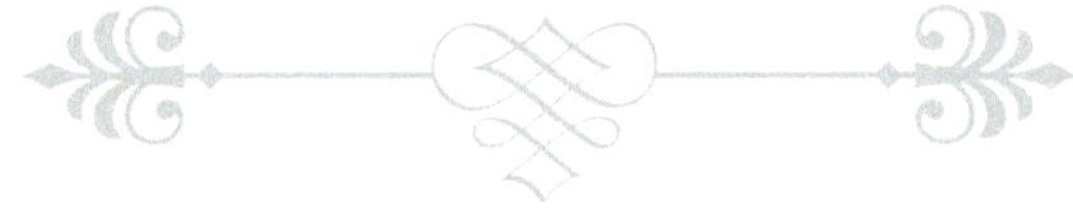

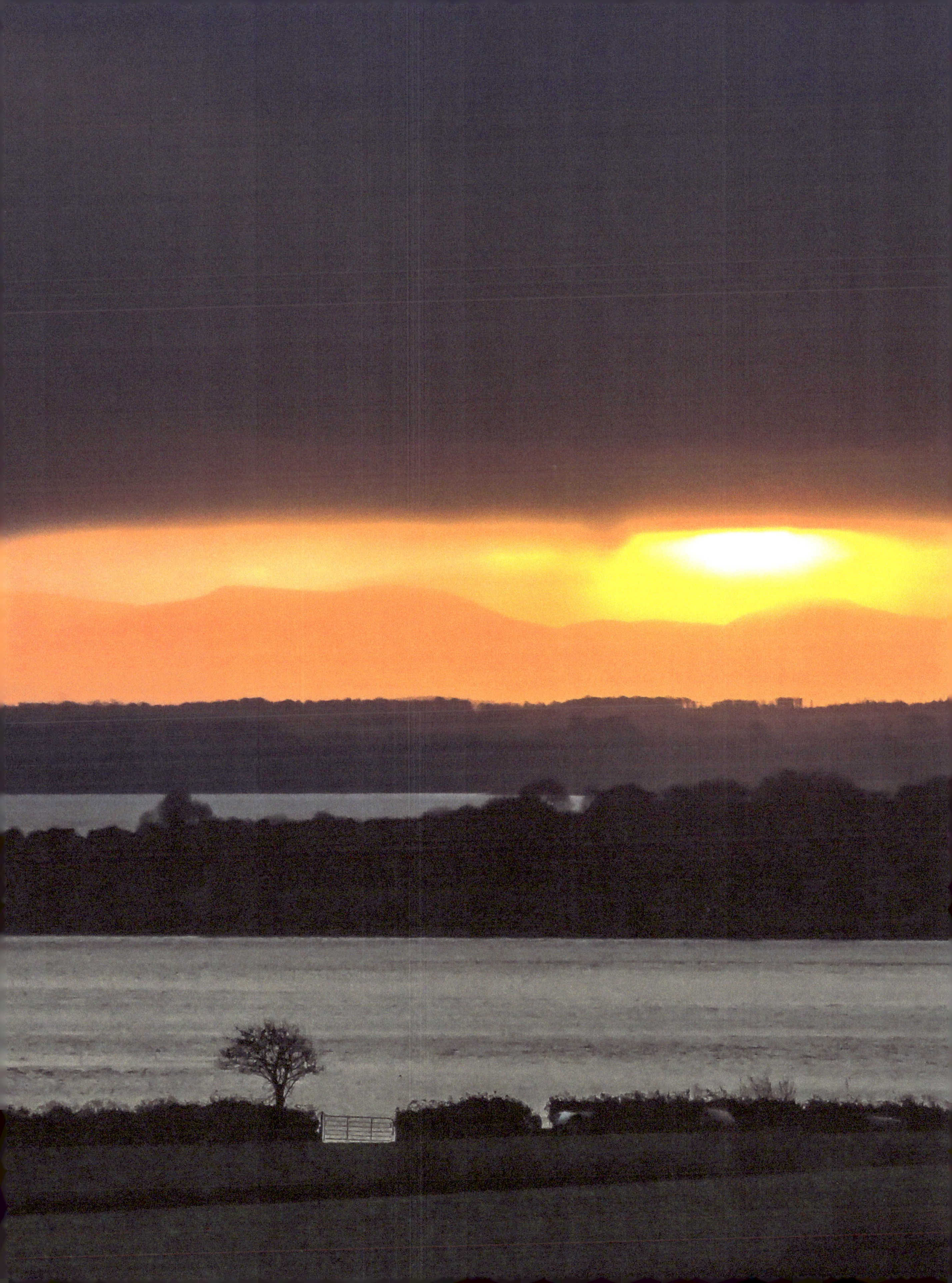

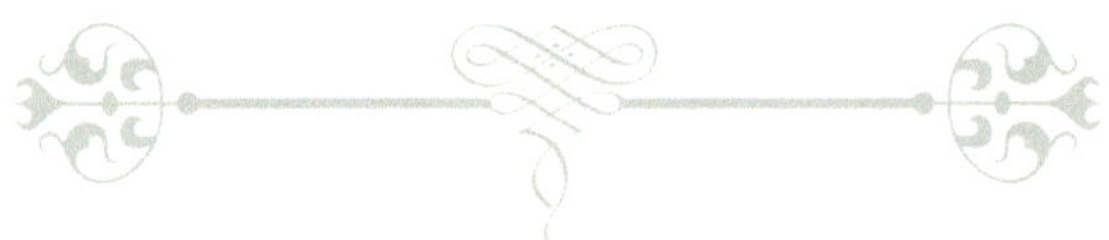

## On the Edge of Morning

**T**hrough the centuries, this section of the Shannon Estuary had Vikings, monks and traders plying its waters. Eventually, freighters took over, and for a time, flying boats used this area for takeoffs and landings. Large tankers and freighters still carry shipments from the Atlantic to the port in Limerick along this route.

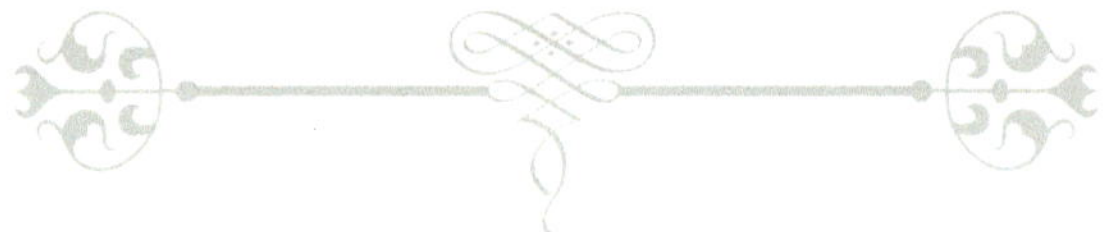

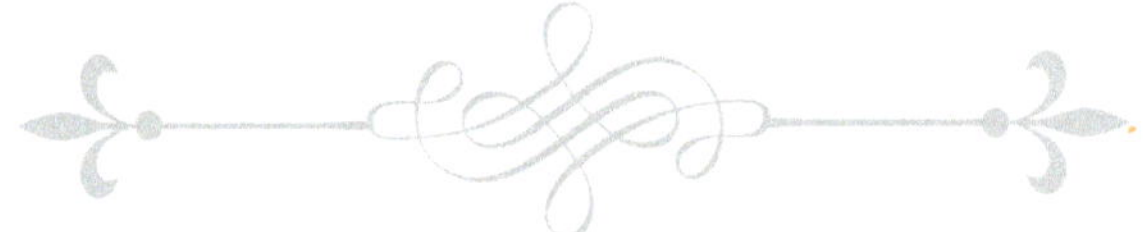

## Brilliant Sunbeams

The sun peeks through clouds as it rises over the Galtee Mountains, a range that stretches through counties Tipperary and Limerick. County Clare has a front-row seat to these majestic sunrises.

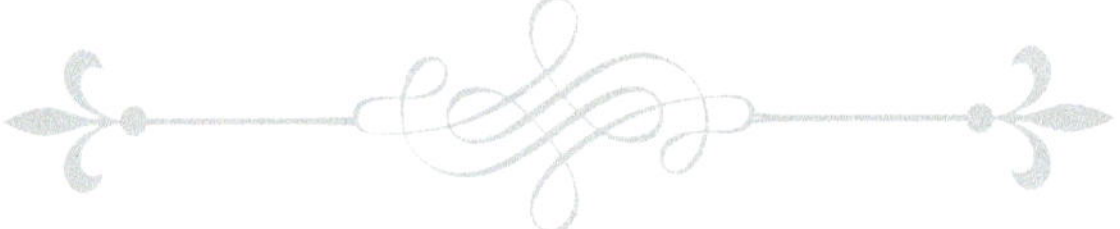

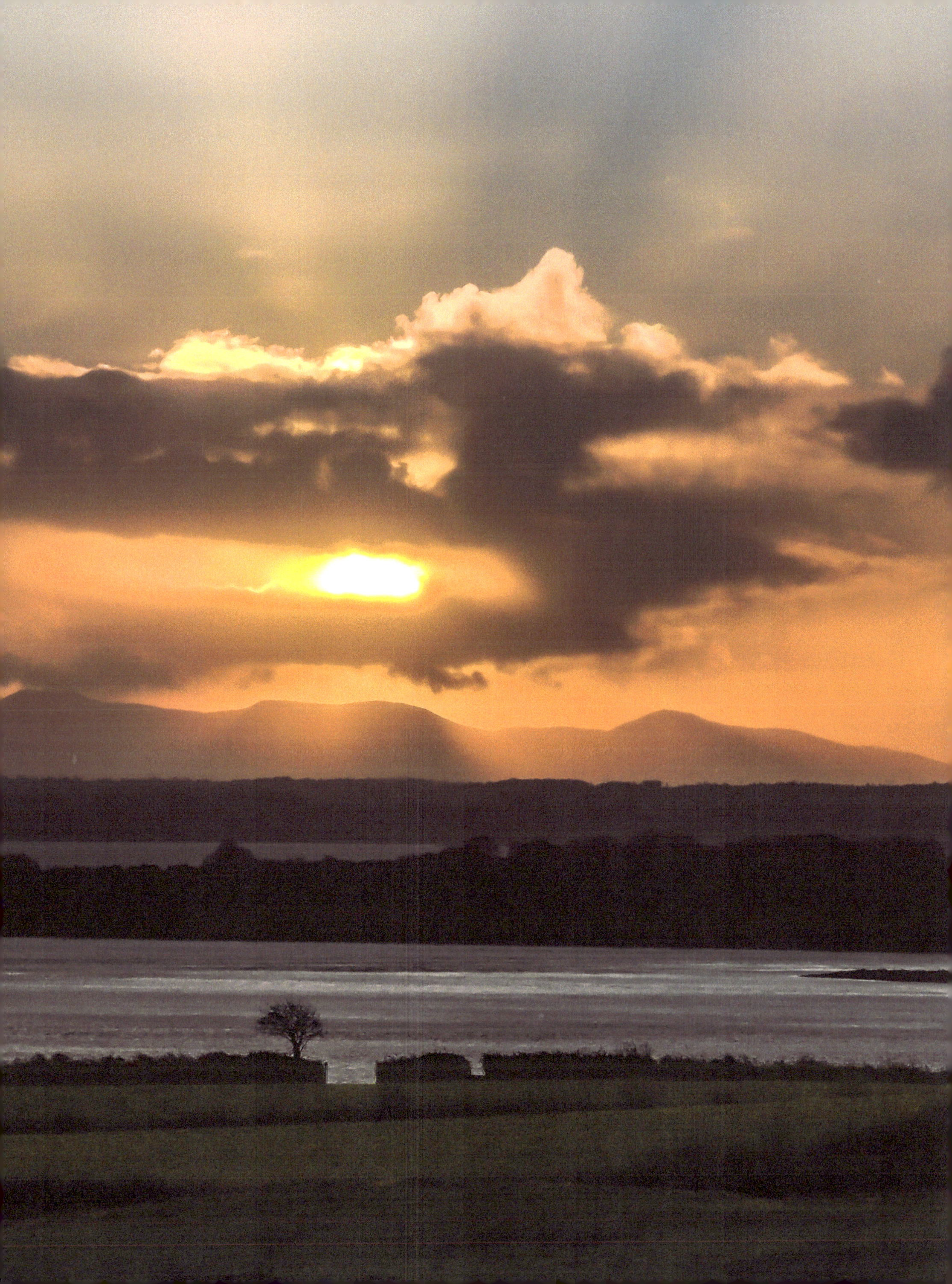

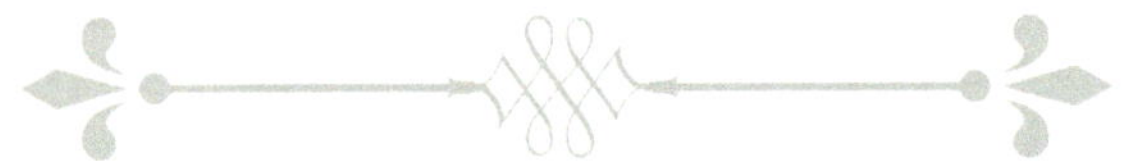

## Cotton Candy Sunrise

A soft pink glow turned these clouds into bundles of cotton candy hanging over the Shannon Estuary one August morning.

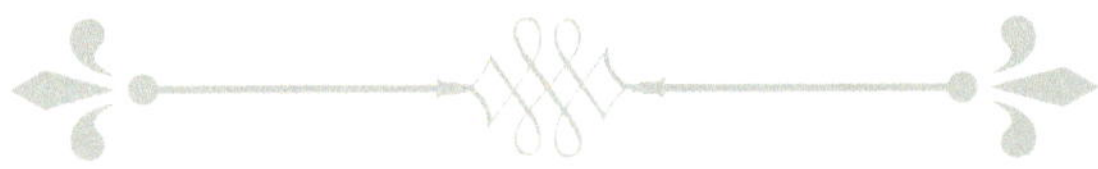

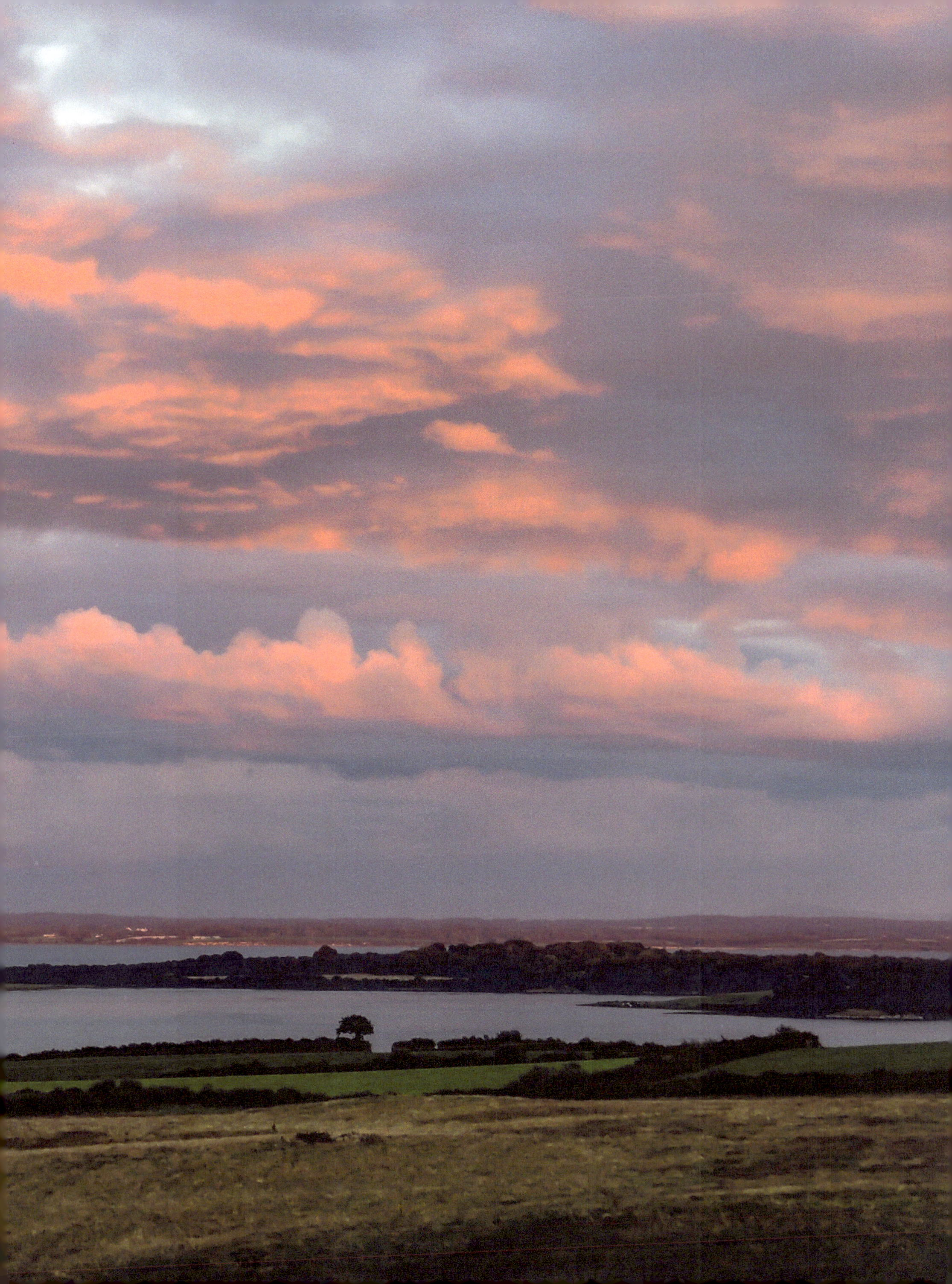

## Galtee Mountains Silhouette

**T**he rising sun silhouettes a section of the Galtee Mountains, Ireland's highest inland mountain range, as a new day begins in the Irish countryside.

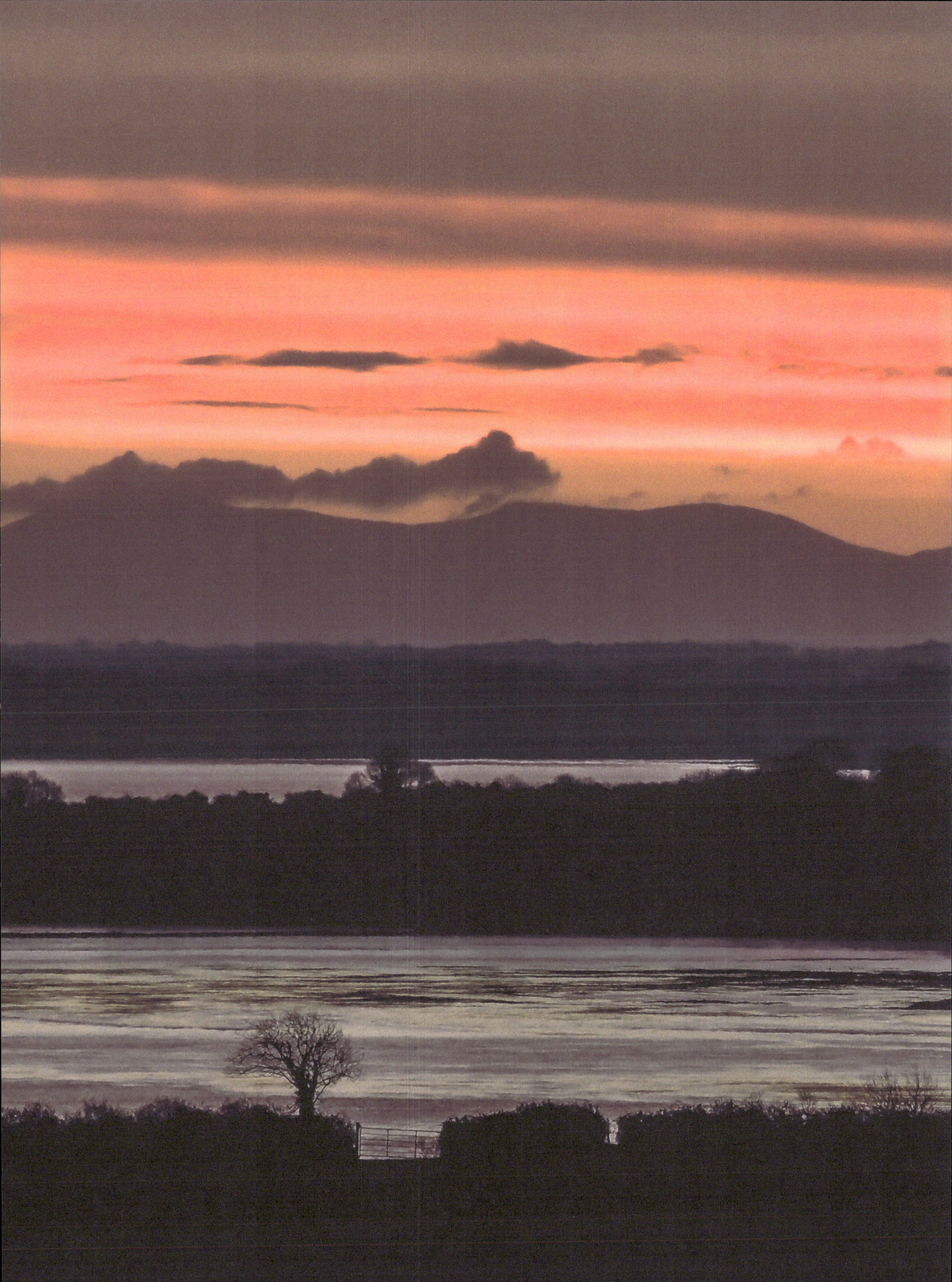

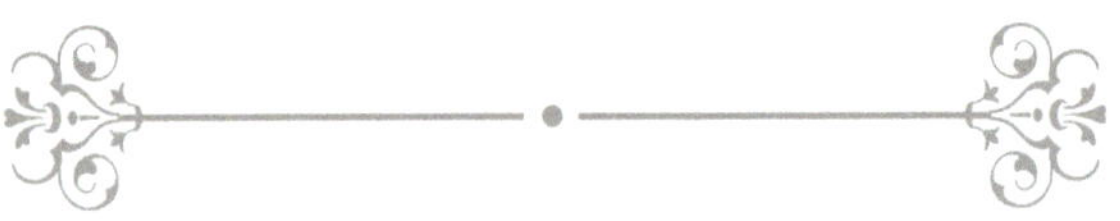

## Intense Orange Sunrise

**T**hese intense sunrises only last for 10 to 15 minutes, but the artistry imprints on the soul... This January sunrise was captured in 2018. I wonder what the ancient inhabitants of Ireland thought of these cosmic spectres. Were they afraid or did they celebrate?

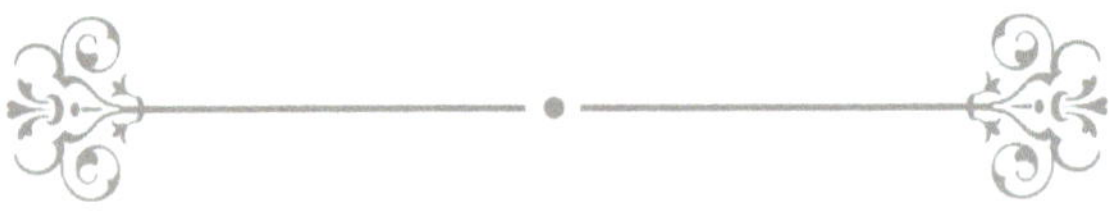

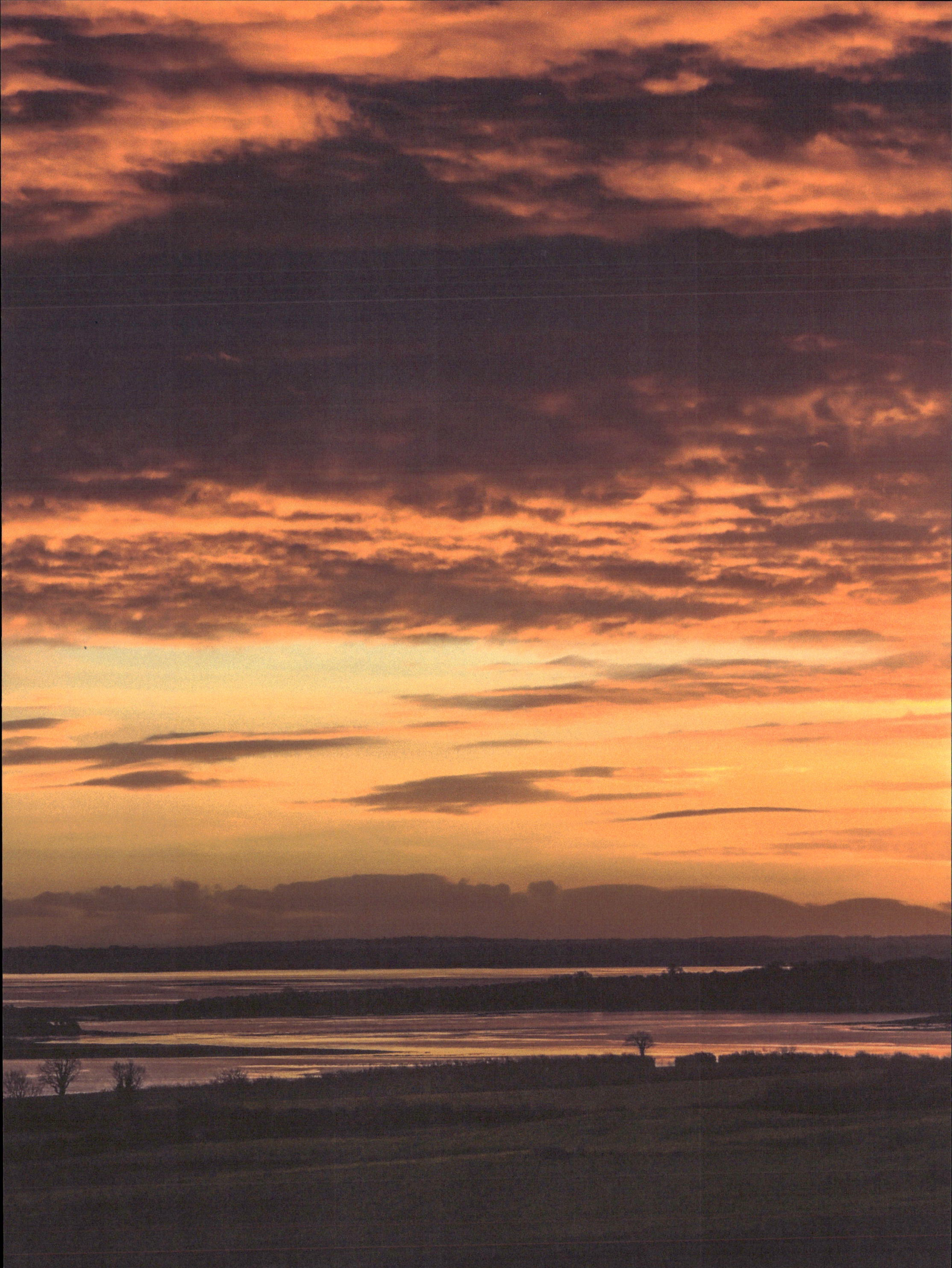

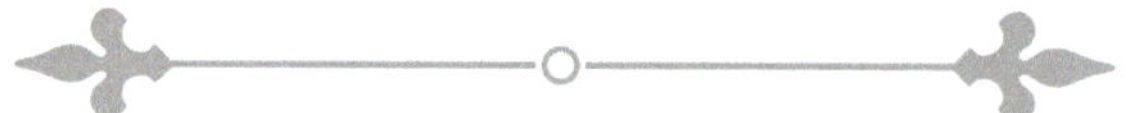

## Ever-Changing Moods

**E**very day, the skies change... the clouds, currents and reflections conspire to express a different mood, always powerful and always beautiful.

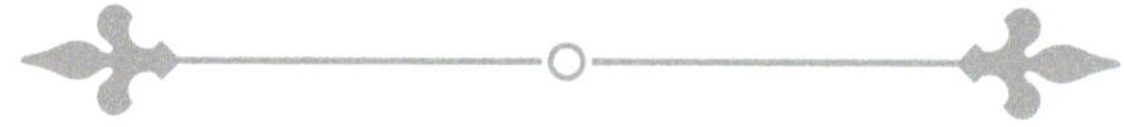

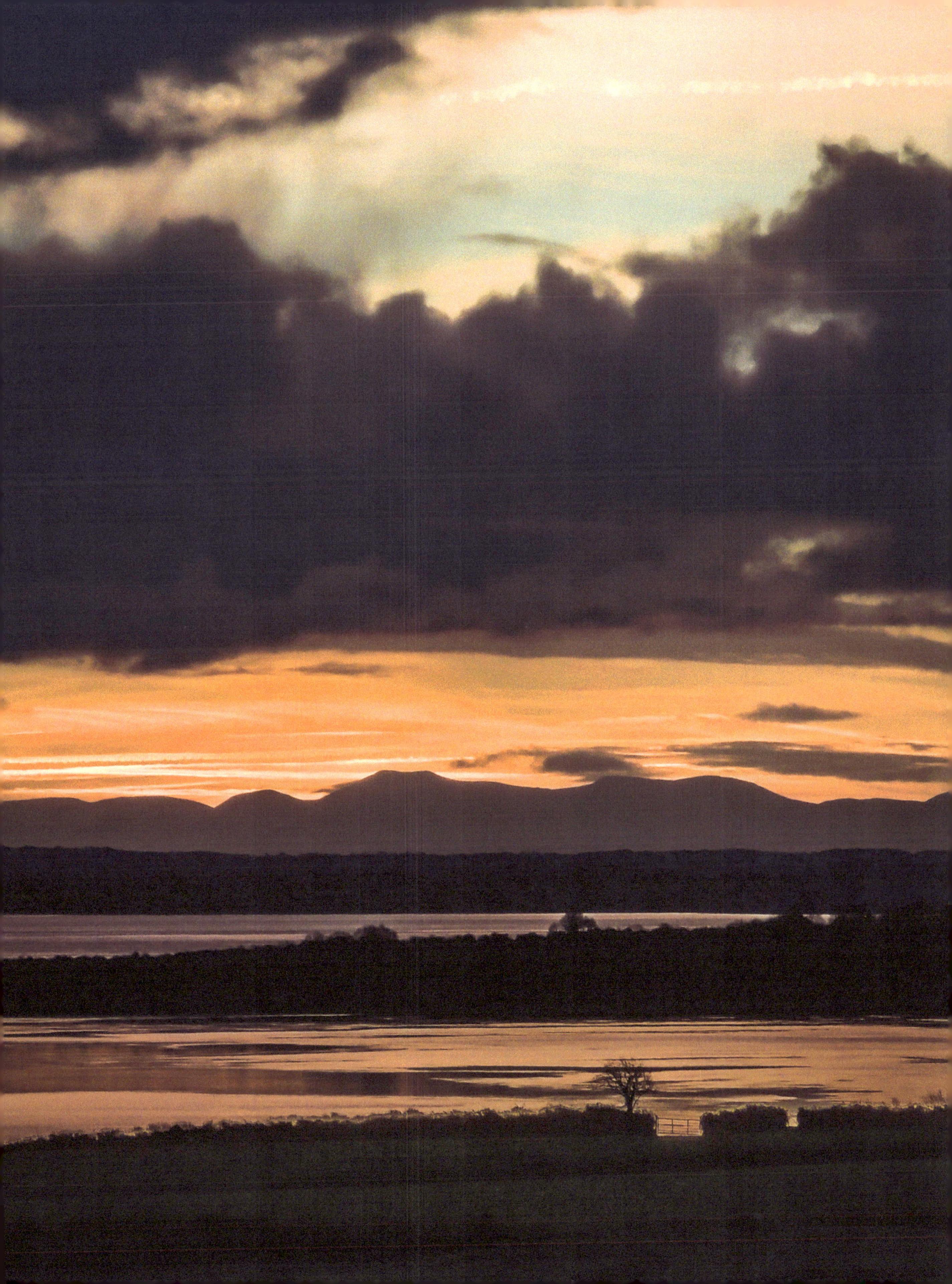

## Summer Wildflowers at Sunrise

**T**hese lovely purple Great Willowherb blossoms brighten the Summer County Clare countryside under an August pastel sunrise.

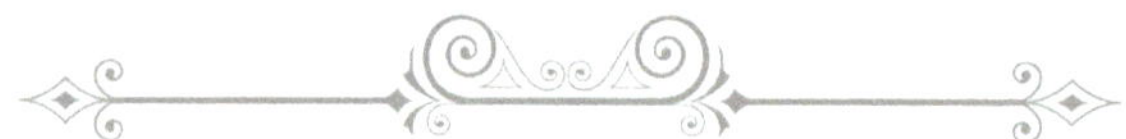

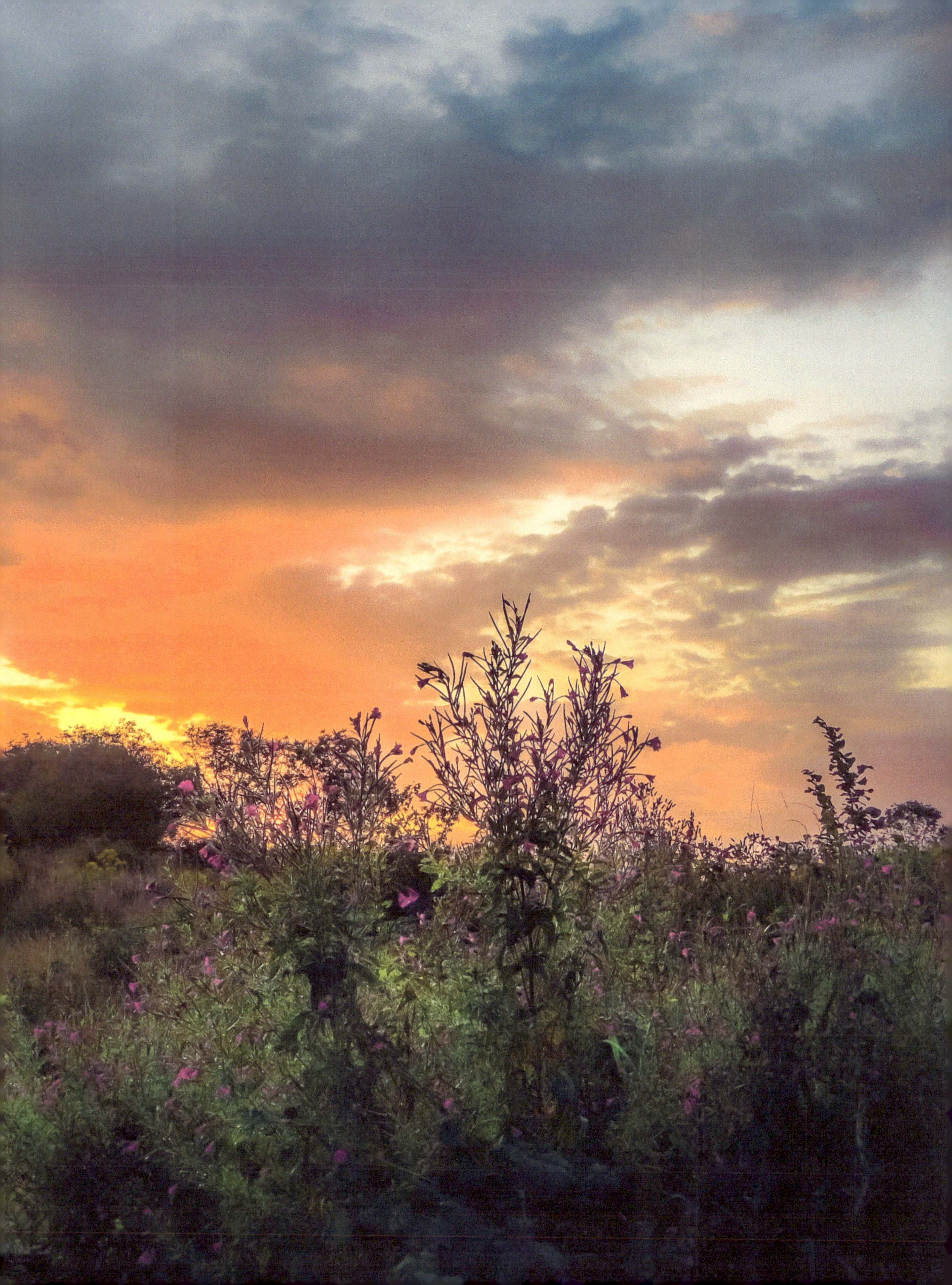

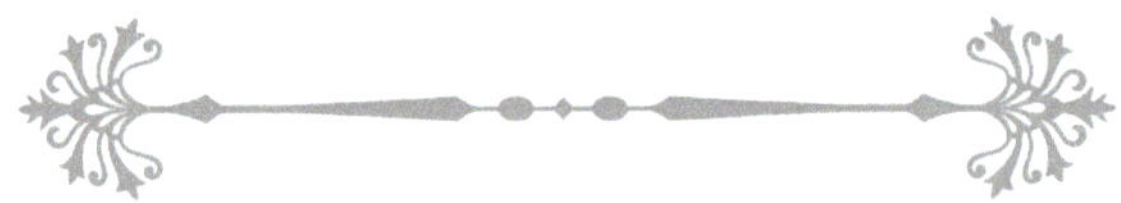

## Sunrise in Winter

**A** sharp December frost attempts to engulf this County Clare meadow, only to be stopped by rays from the rising sun.

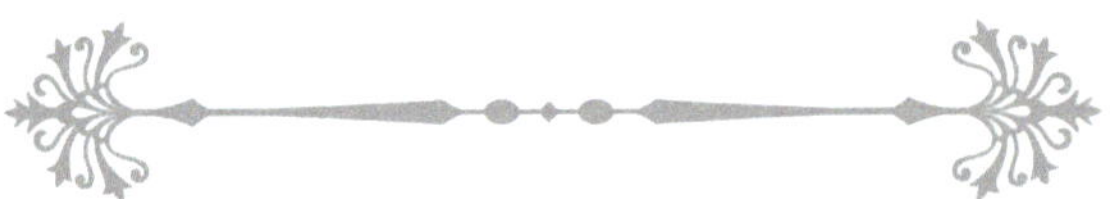

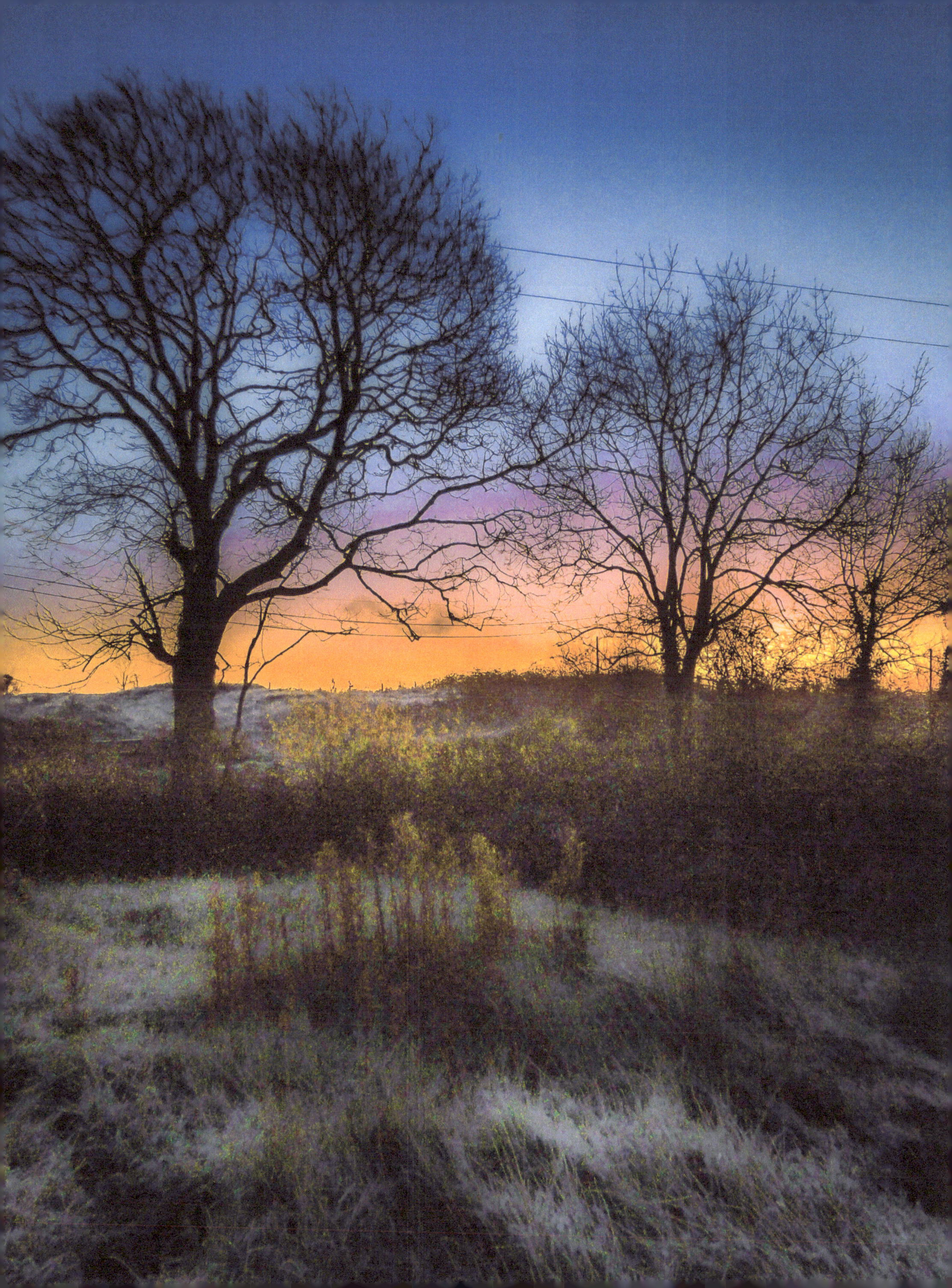

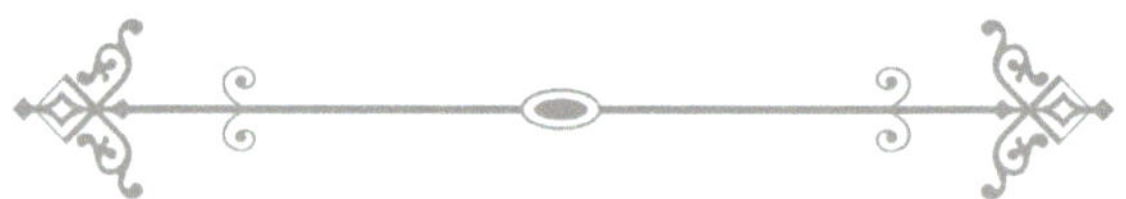

## Foggy Winter Sunrise

**A** bank of fog attempts to obstruct the boiling sky from reaching the frozen pasture below on the shores of the Shannon Estuary at Crovraghan, County Clare.

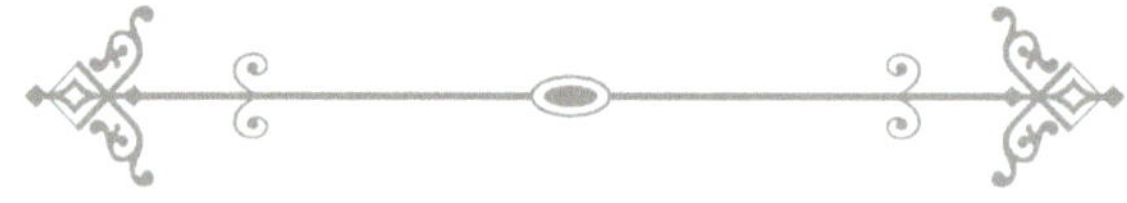

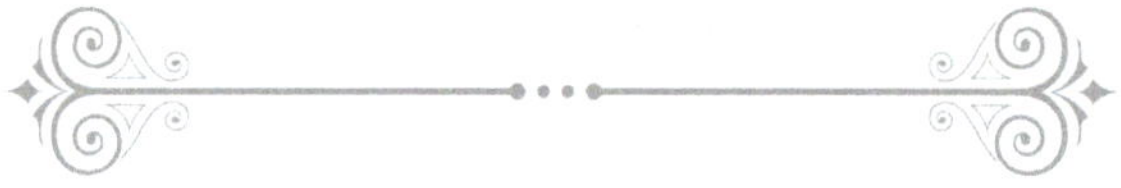

## Sunrise Ice Reflections

**P**atterns crafted by an overnight freeze on my car's windshield reflect the yellow light from the rising sun in February 2019. Nature's artistry at its best!

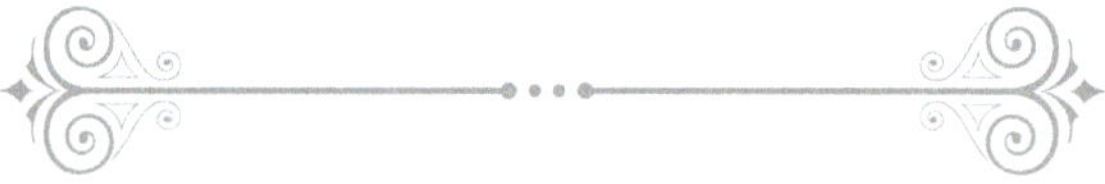

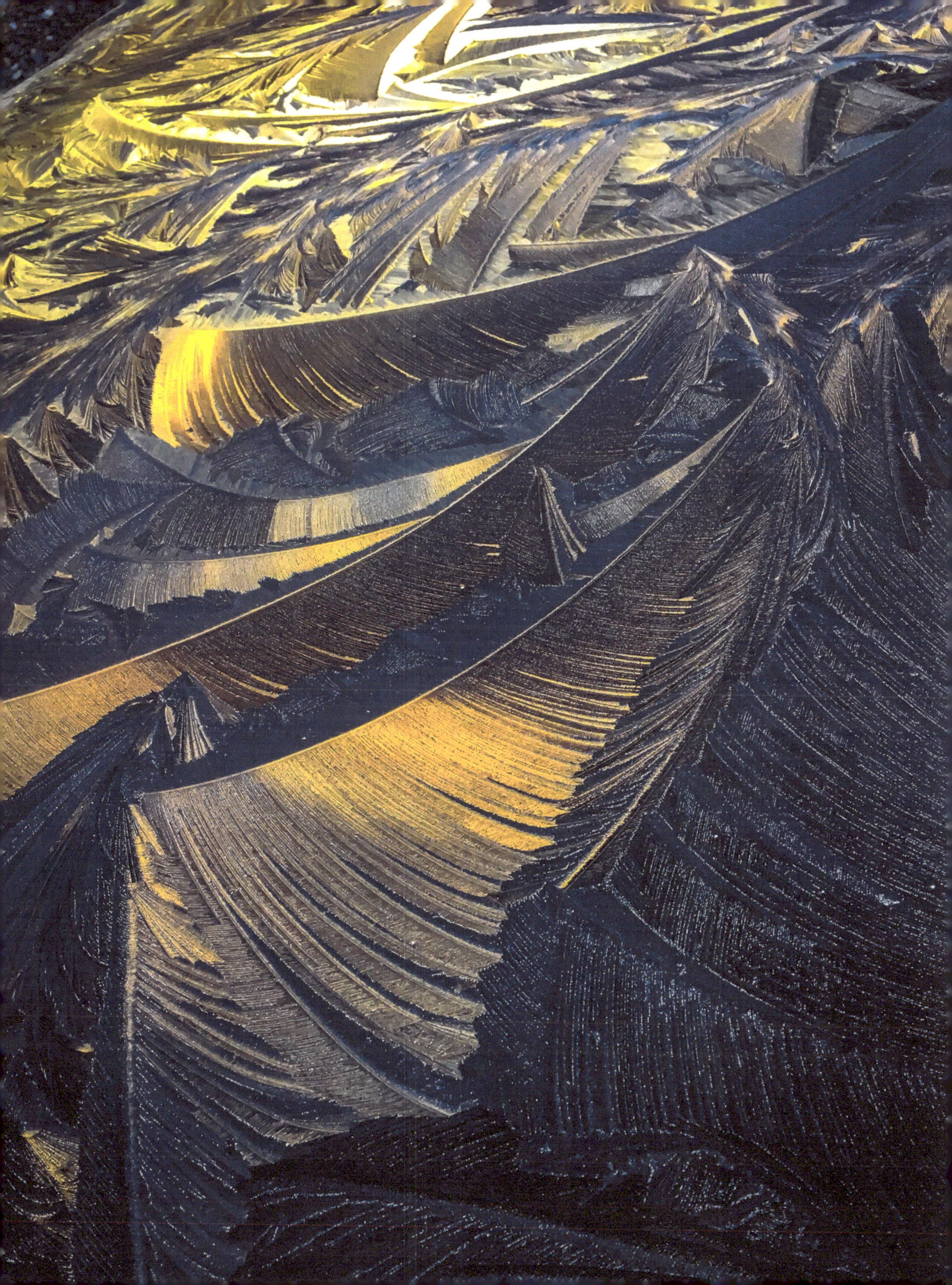

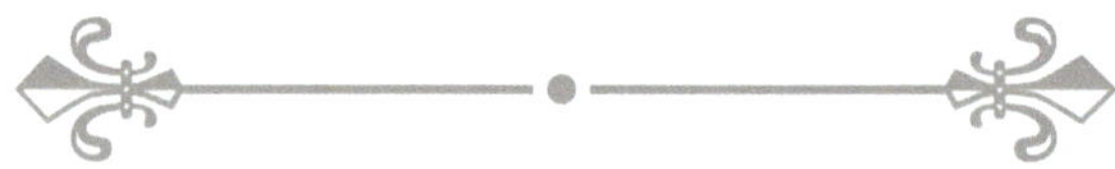

## Sunrise Breaking Through Cold Front

The February sun shines through cloud cover to illuminate a portion of the Shannon Estuary — its frozen shores awaiting rebirth in Spring.

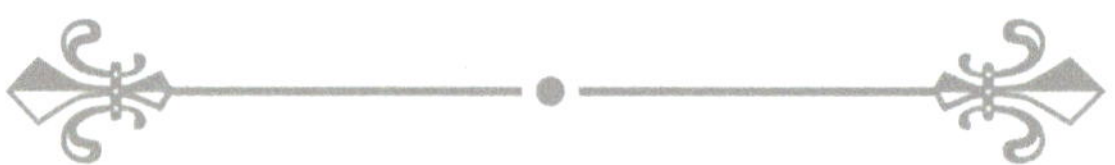

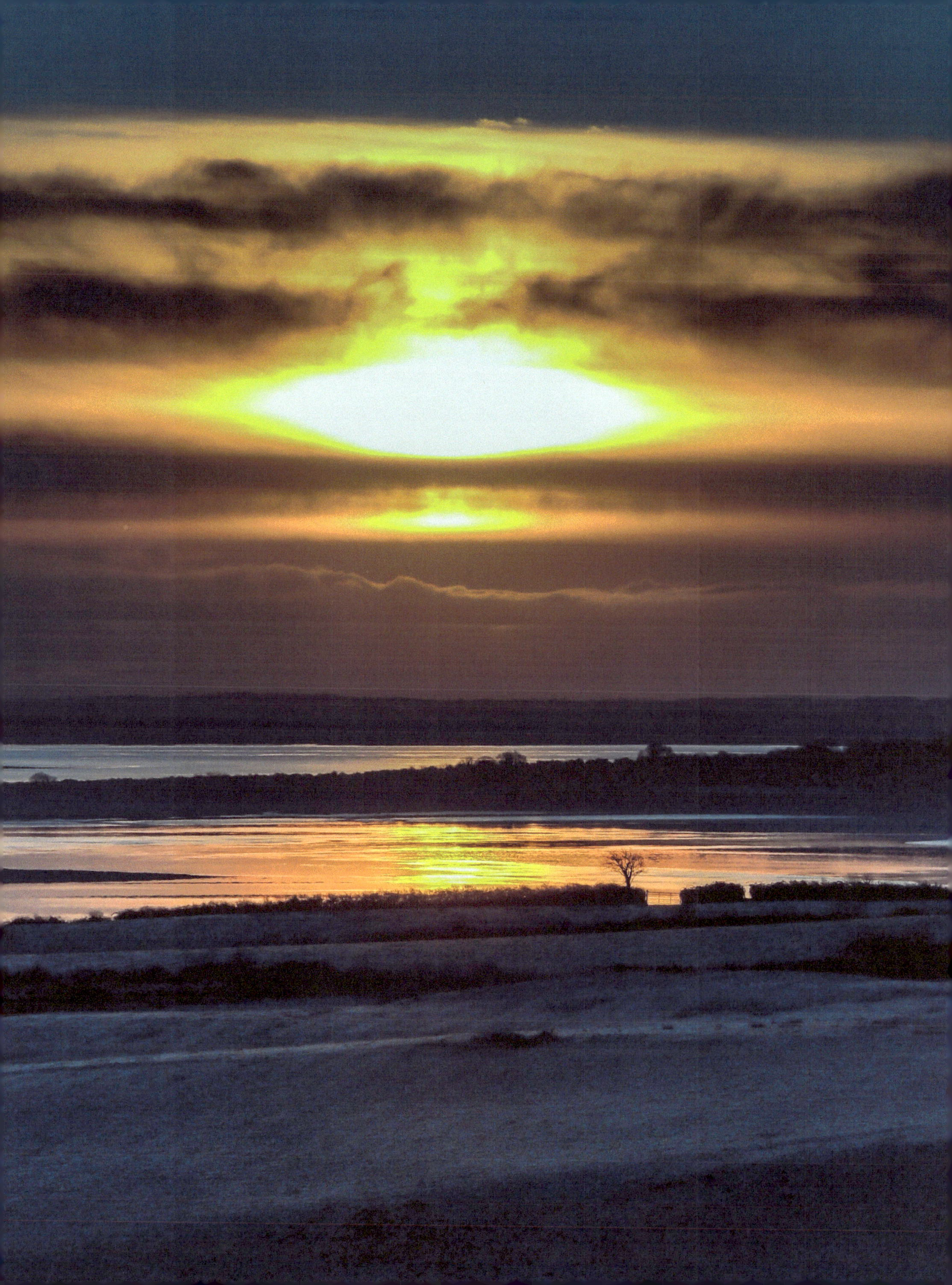

## Spring Sunrise Celebration

**A**s Spring weather begins to transform pastures along the Shannon Estuary, sunrises become more intense and celebratory.

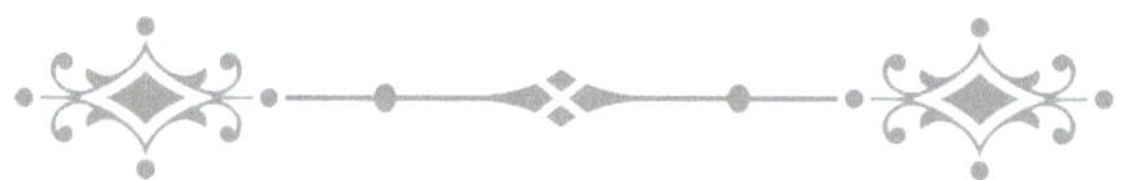

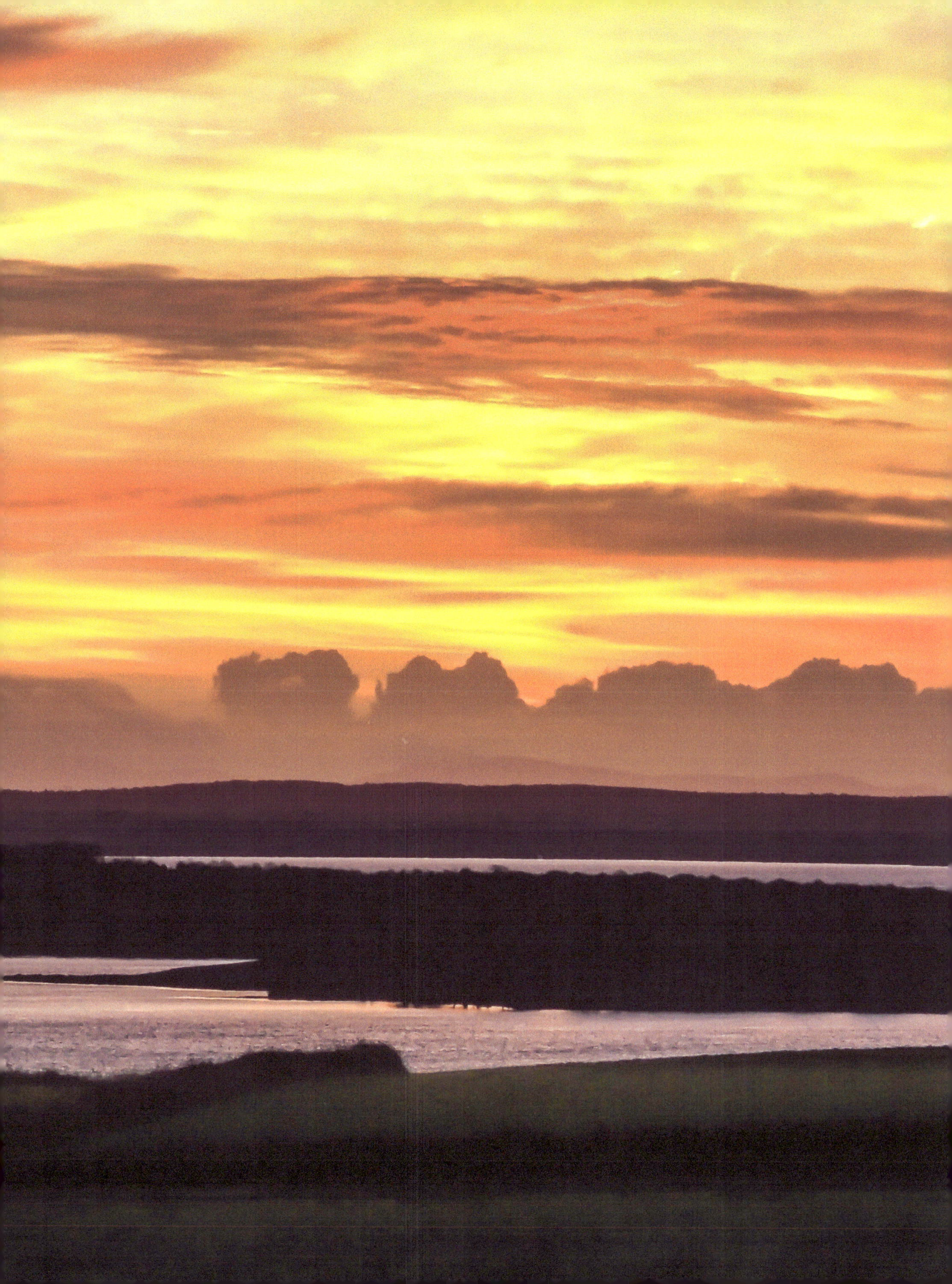

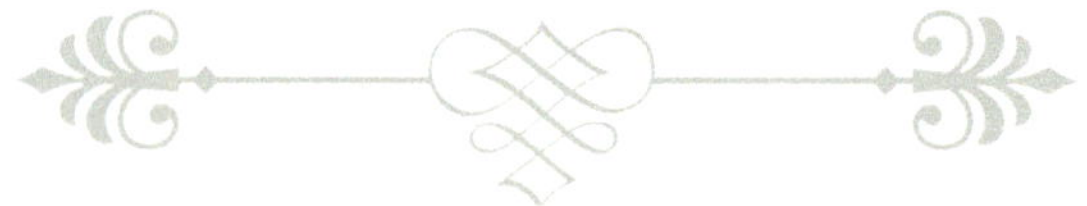

## Spring Sunrise and Daffodils

**D**affodils are among the first Spring wildflower arrivals here in the Irish countryside. The combination of flowers and the emotive sunrises offer many moments of morning tranquility. This image was captured in March 2016.

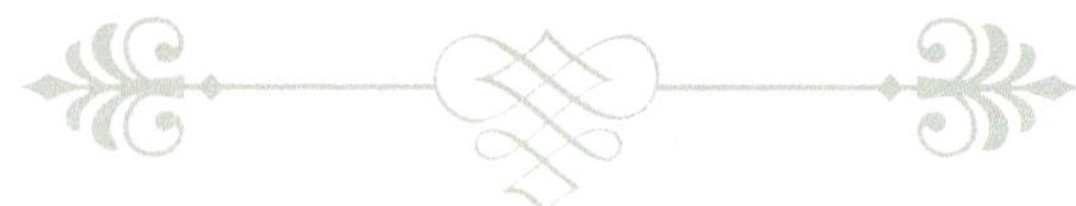

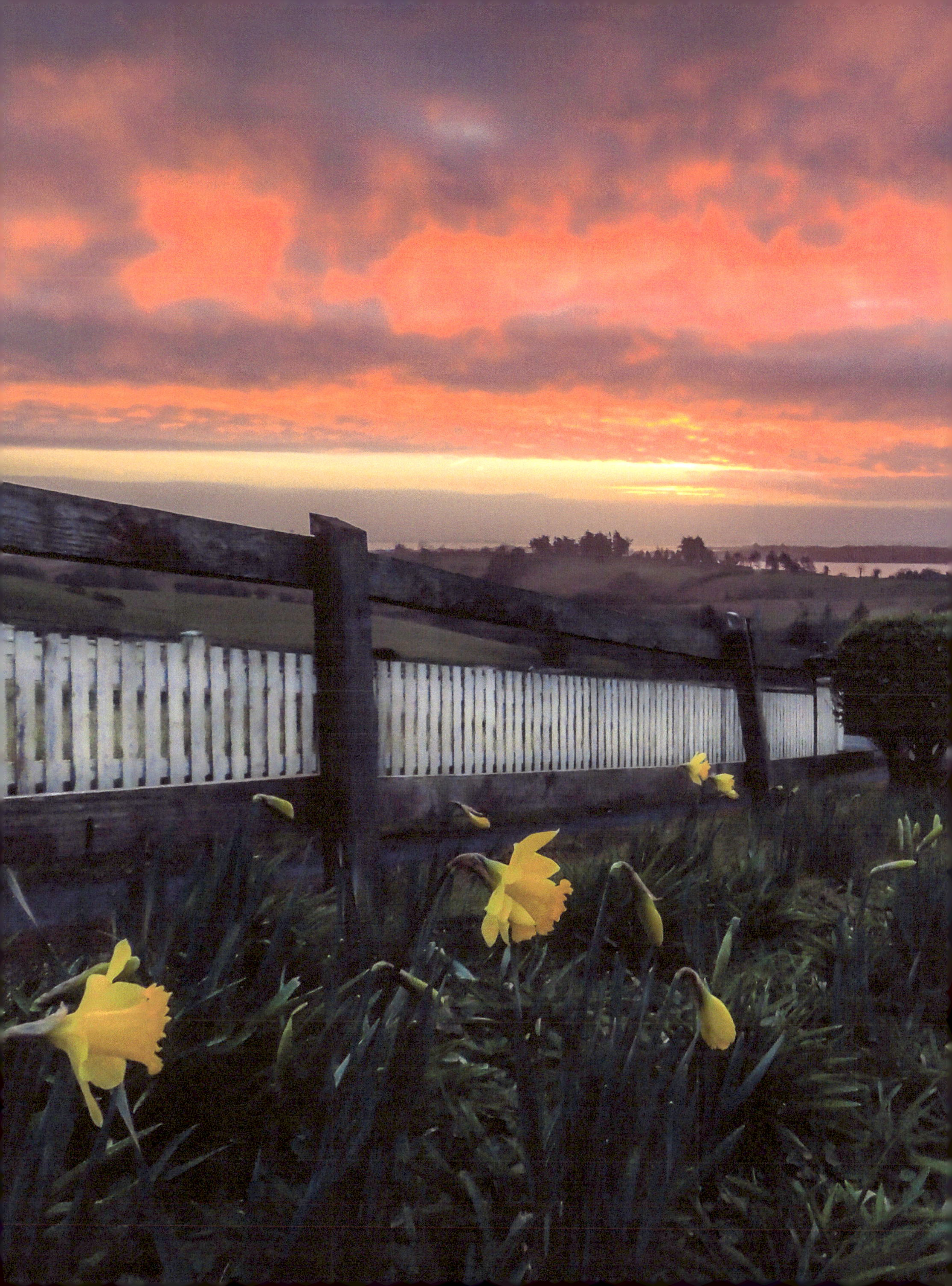

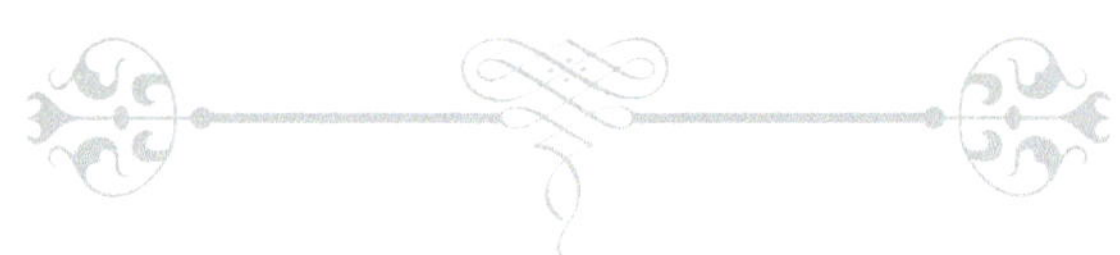

## Sun-kissed Spring Daffodils

**S**un rays gently caress these newly blooming Daffodils at sunrise in late February 2018, with the rolling hills of County Clare as a backdrop.

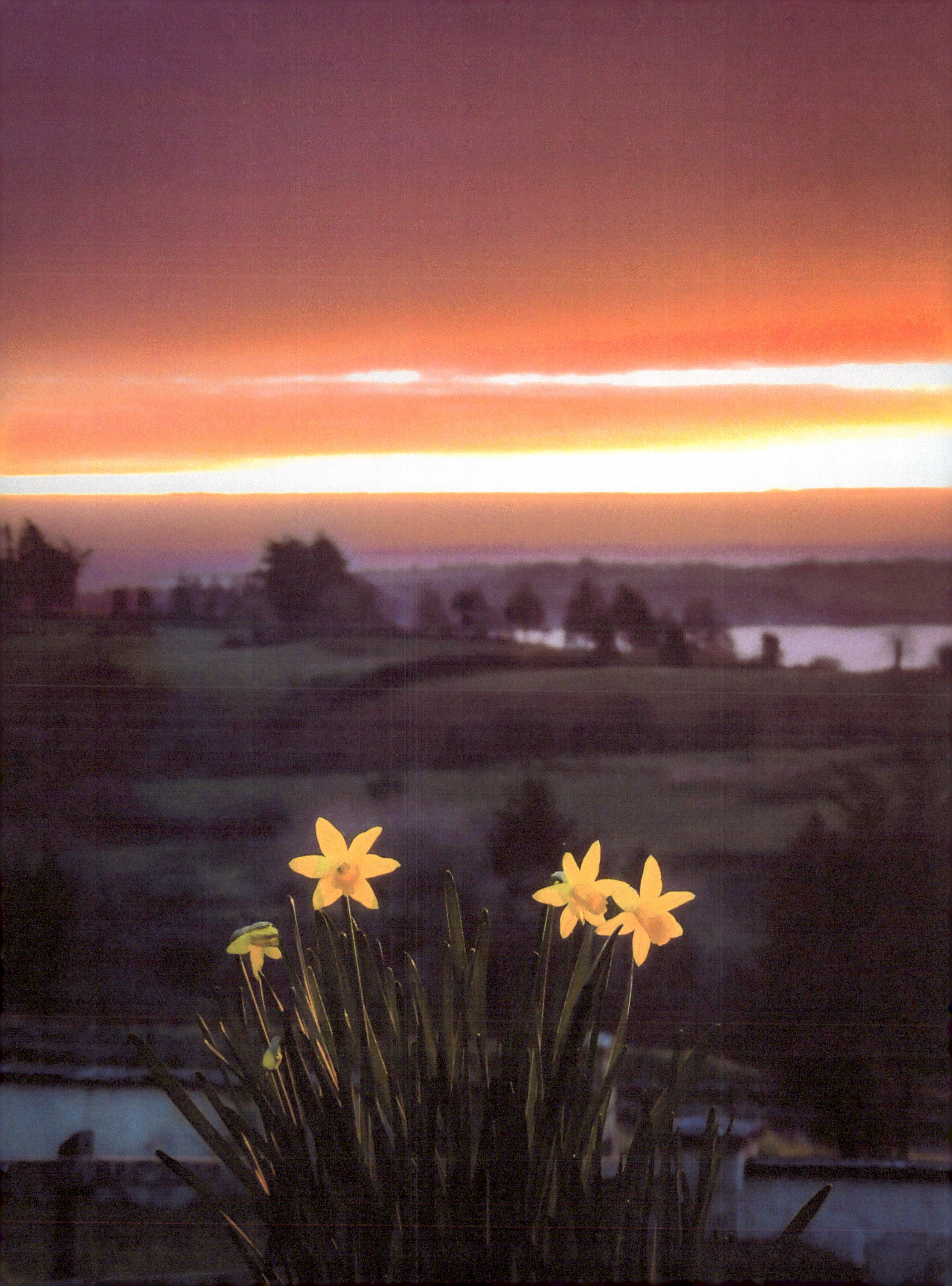

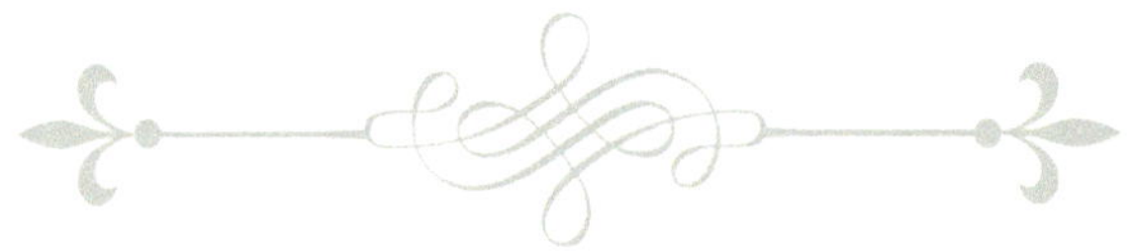

## Somber Sunrise

**A** pinkish glow is captured in the waters of Ireland's Shannon Estuary between islands that once were inhabited by many farming families as well as a monks at a 12th Century Augustinian monastery. This image was captured in May 2016.

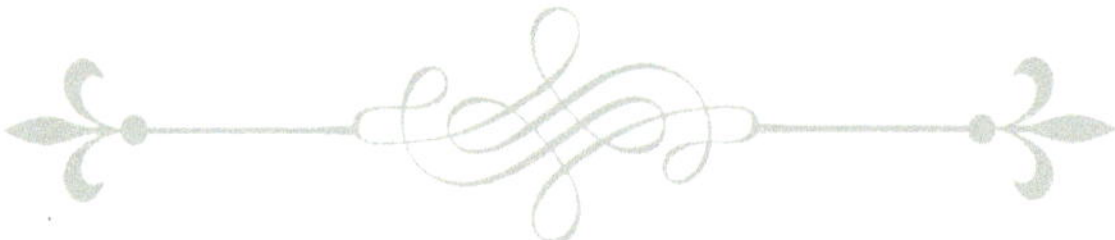

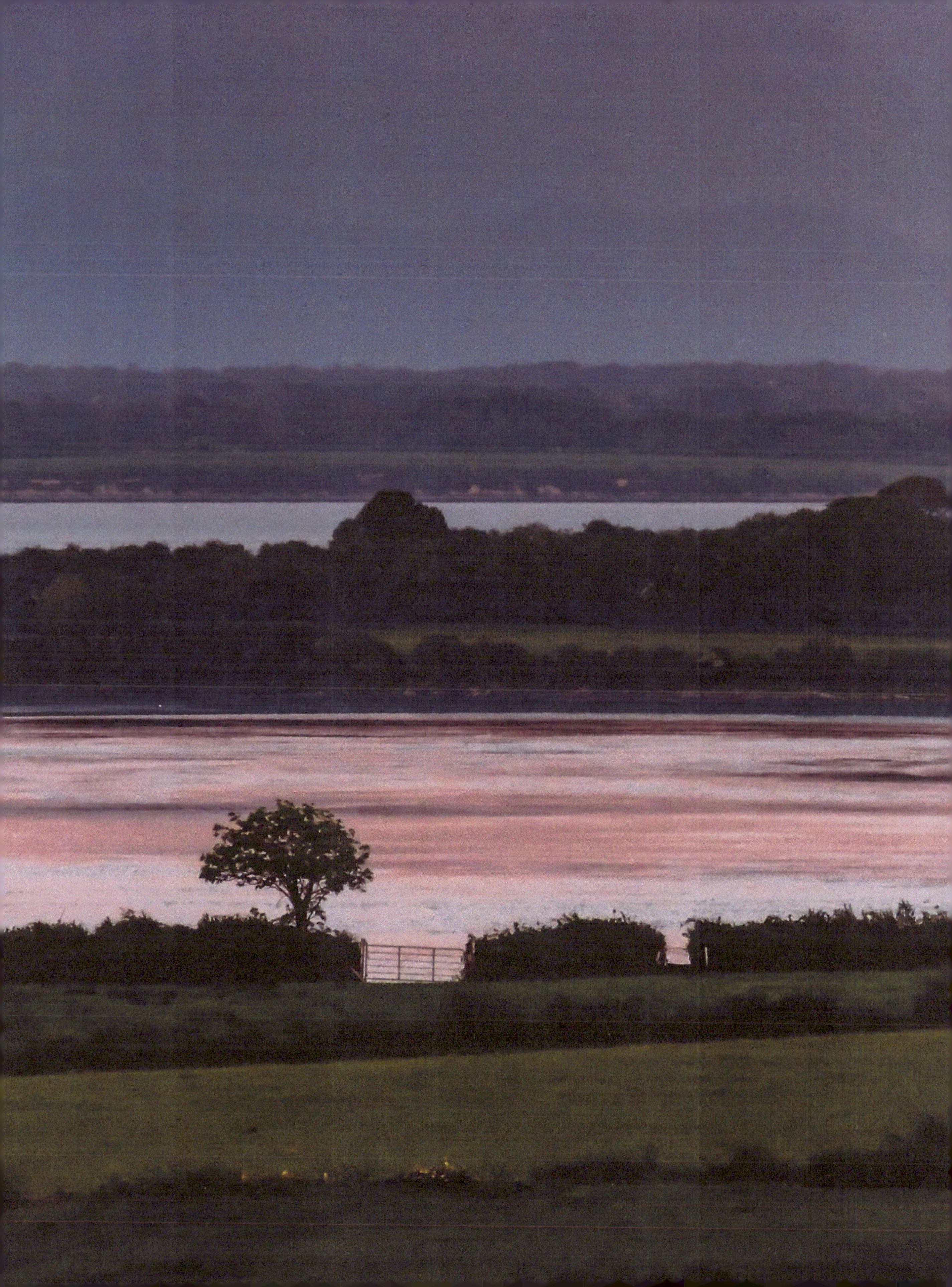

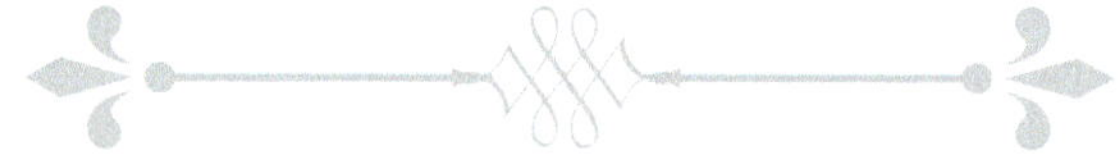

## Misty Morning on the Shannon Estuary

**A**delicate mist rises over the pastures of the townland of Crovraghan near Kildysart, County Clare, as this late August sunrise paints an orange glow above.

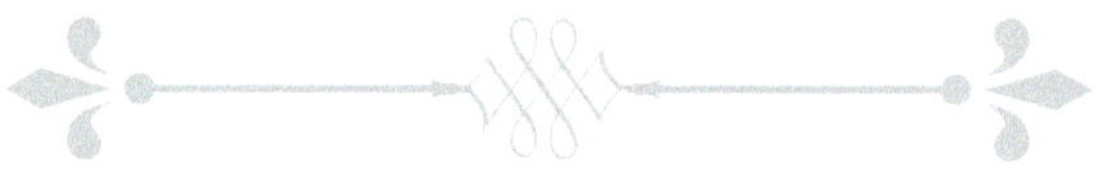

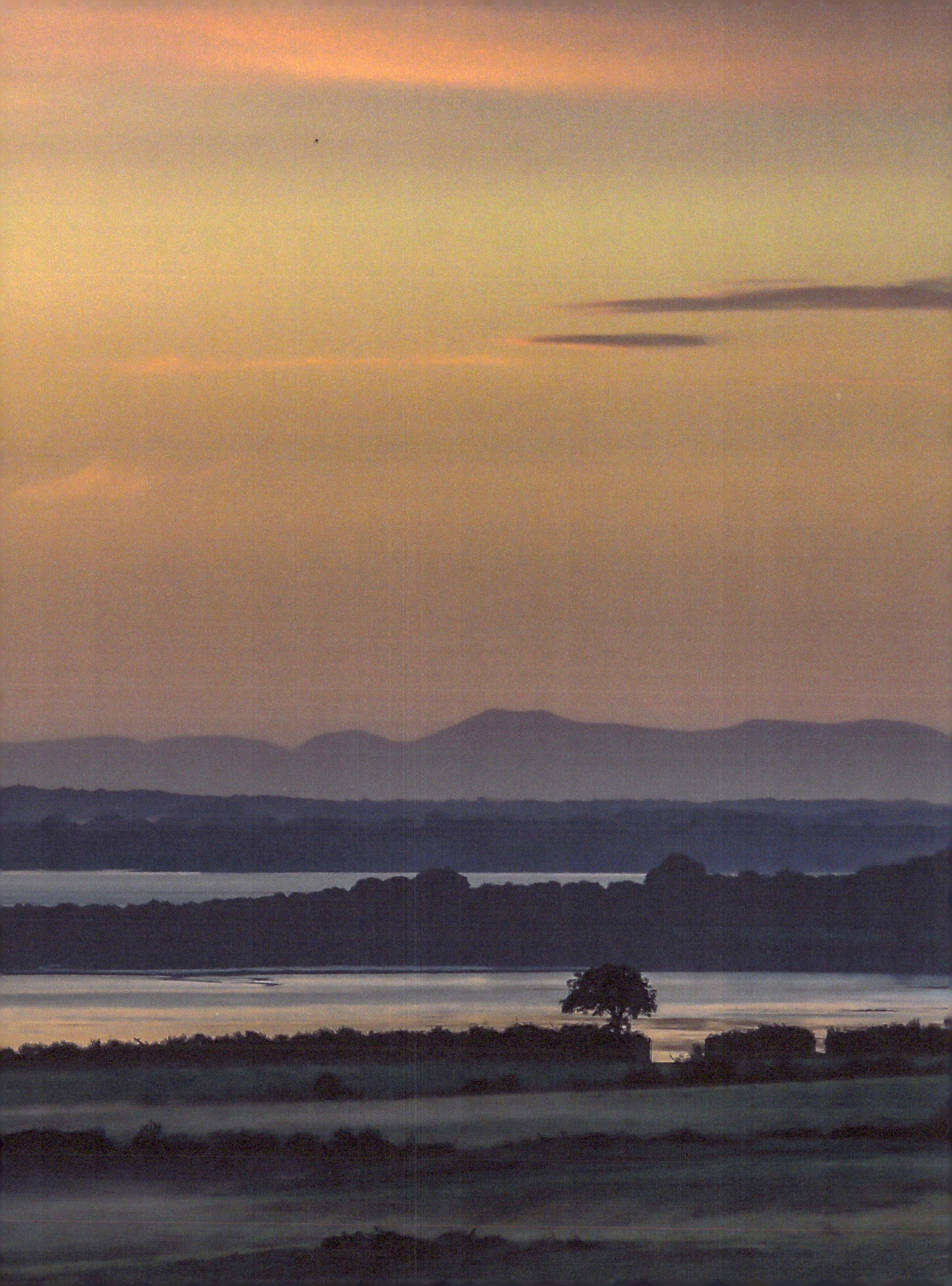

## Different Day, Different Mood

**F**rom day to day, the mercurial sky coupled with the changing seasons bestow a completely different mood and new vision from the same viewpoint in the rolling hills of County Clare. This image was captured in  September 2016.

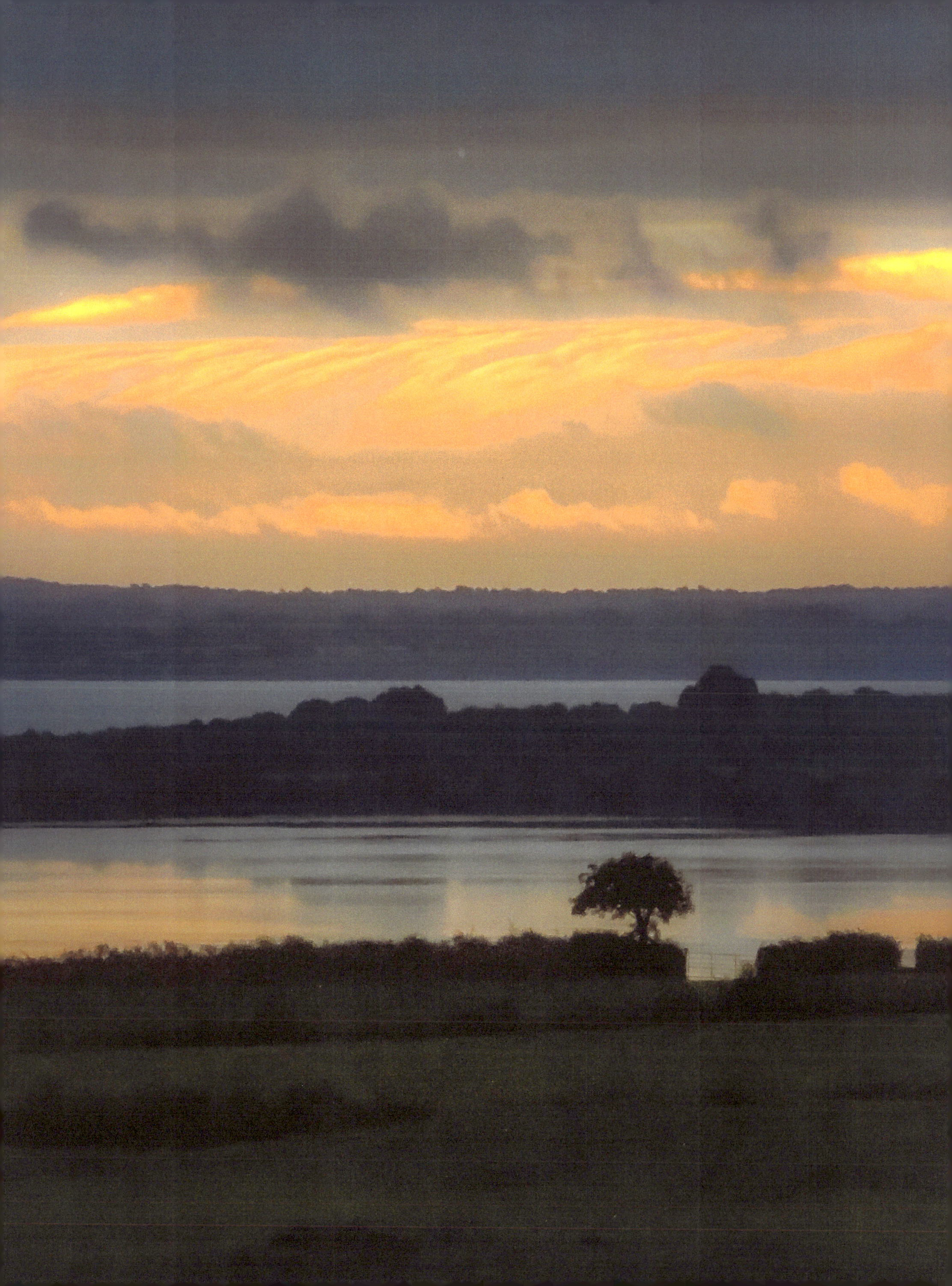

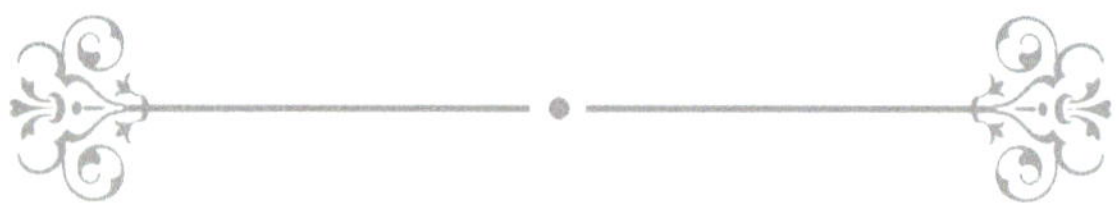

## Reflections of Clare and Limerick

An orange-yellow sky illuminates the Irish country-side and reflects in the calm waters of the Shannon Estuary during an October 2016 sunrise. In the foreground are the shores of County Clare, and in the background are the Galtee Mountains looming over the shores of County Limerick.

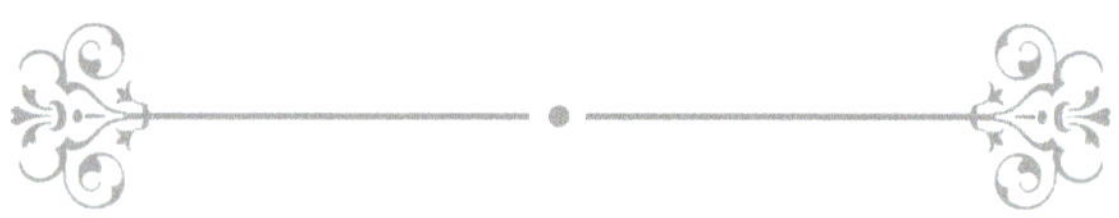

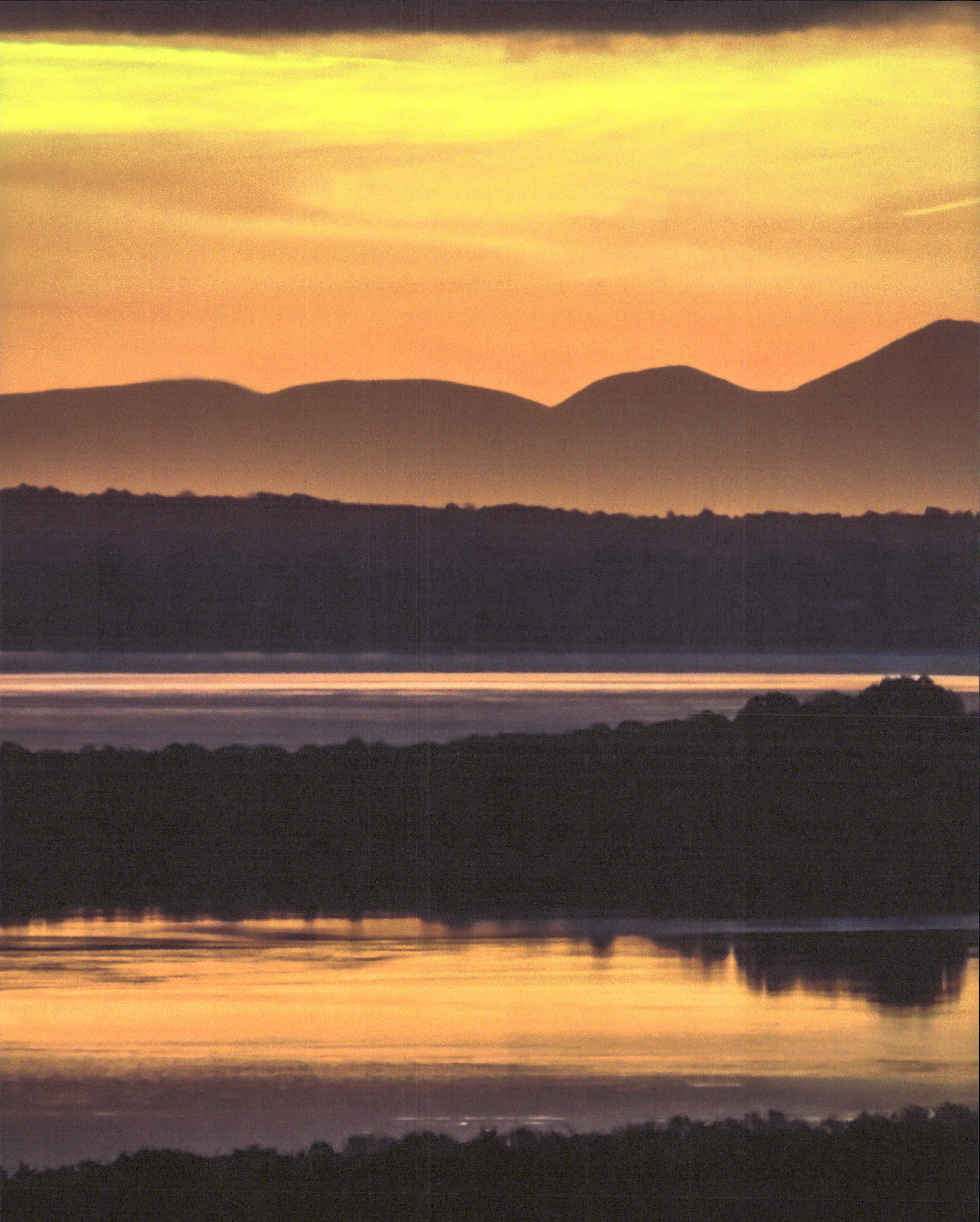

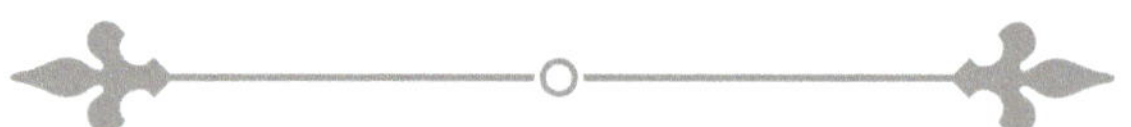

## Misty Orange January Sunrise

**L**ow tide reveals a land-bridge between islands in the Shannon Estuary during this misty orange sunrise captured in January 2017.

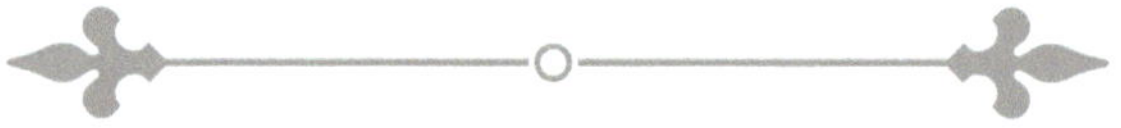

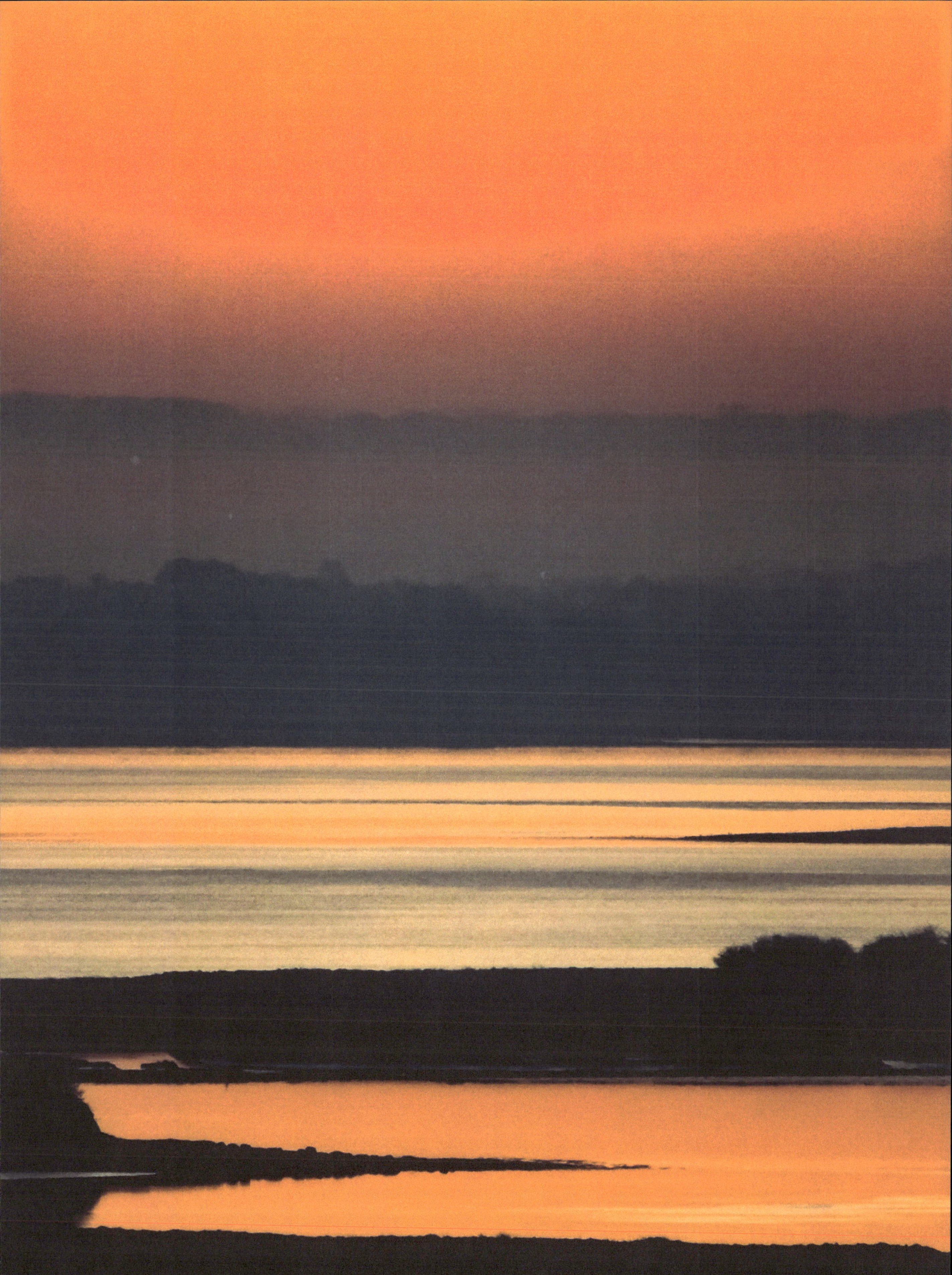

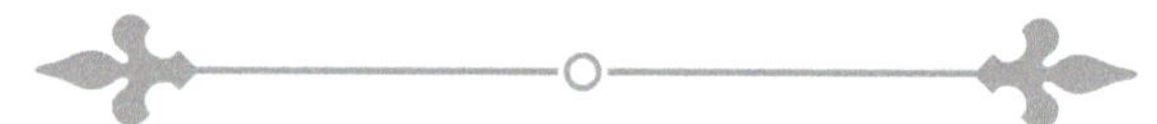

## Crisp Winter Sky Reflections

**A**lone light shines from the distant shores of County Limerick as a gradually lightening crisp Winter sky reflects in the Shannon Estuary.

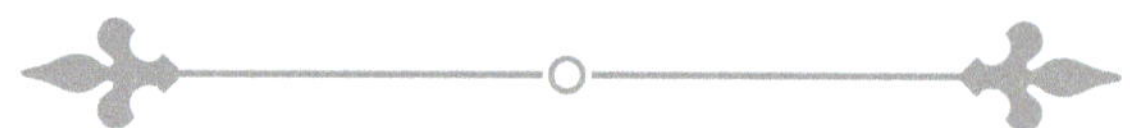

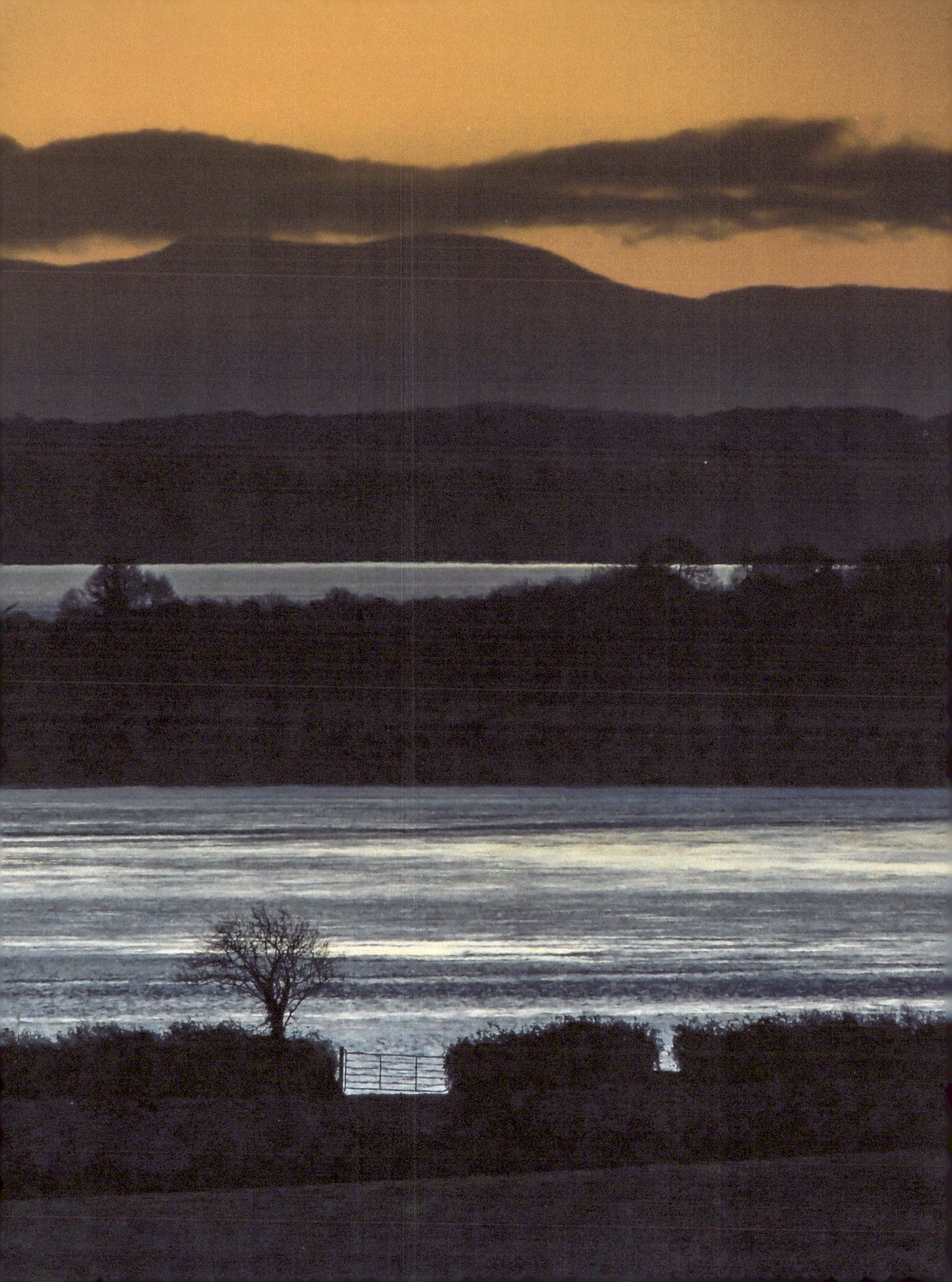

## Early Autumn Sunrise

A gentle pink sunrise illuminates the underside of a cloud bank in this image captured in September 2017 over the Shannon Estuary.

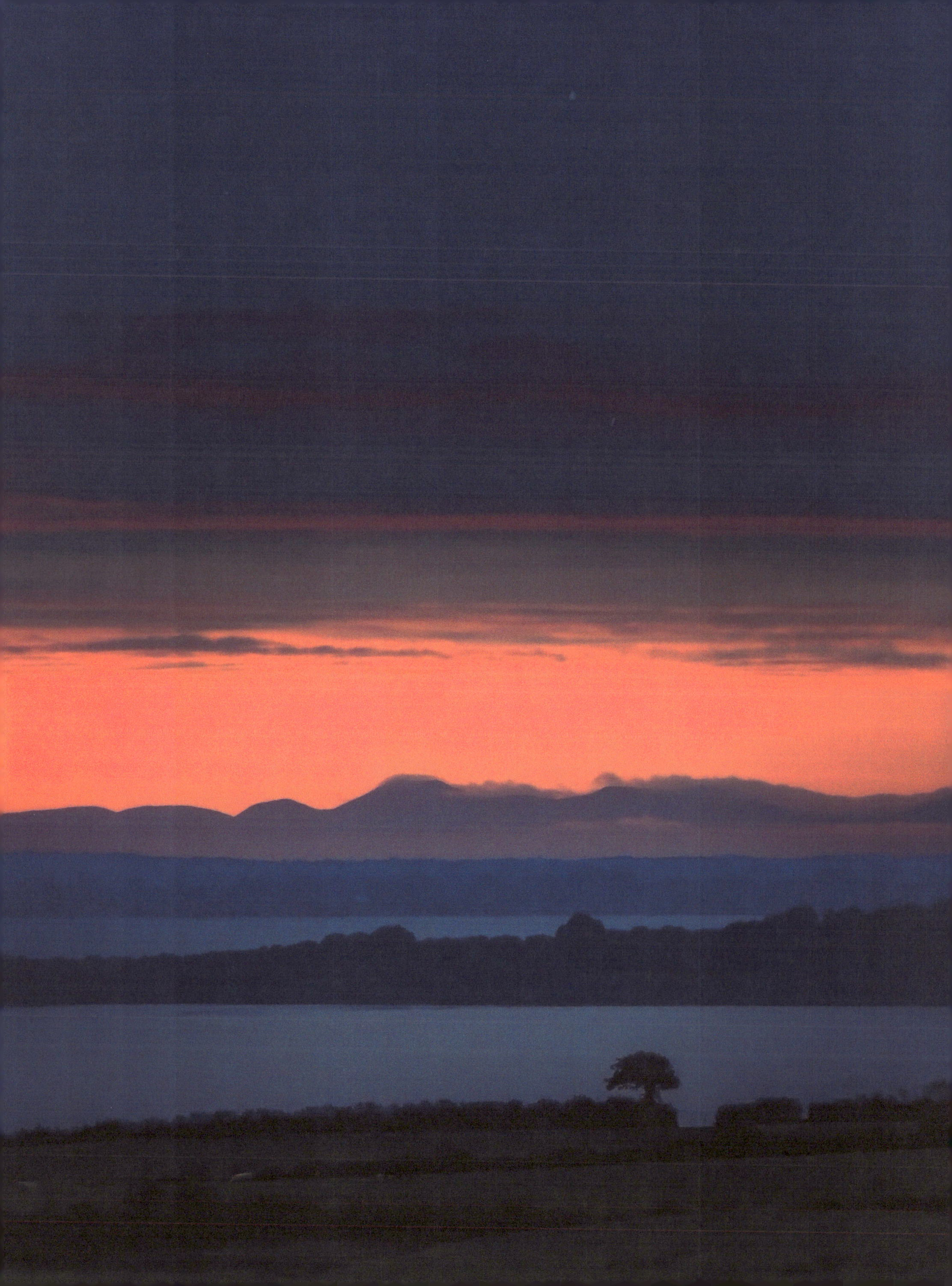

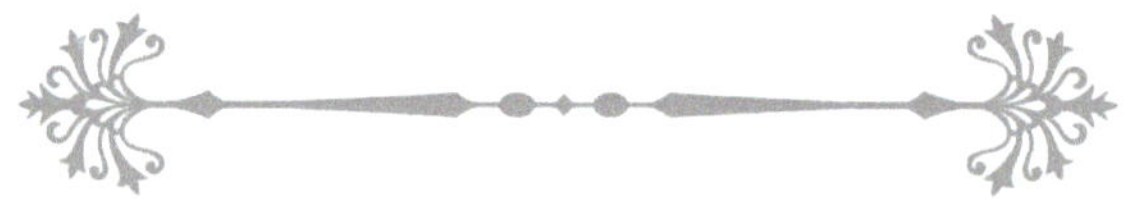

## Battle of Clouds and Sunbeams

As the seasons progress, the battle between impending Winter weather and sunbeams intensifies. This November sunrise illustrates the challenge as dark clouds attempt to block the emerging rays.

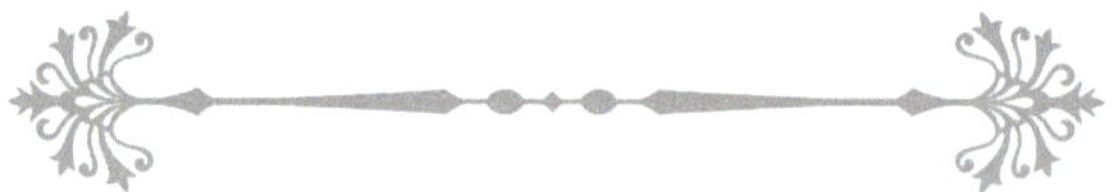

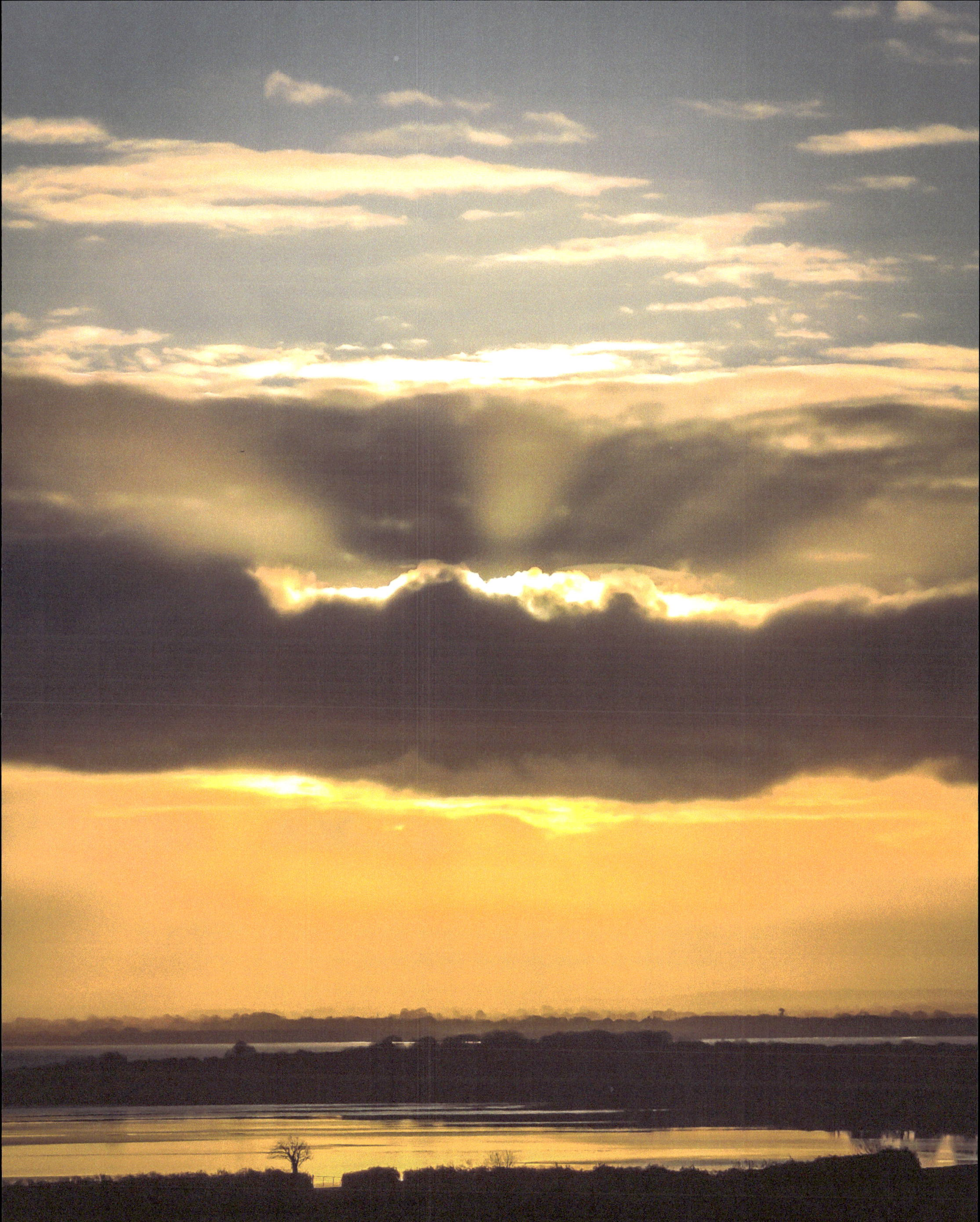

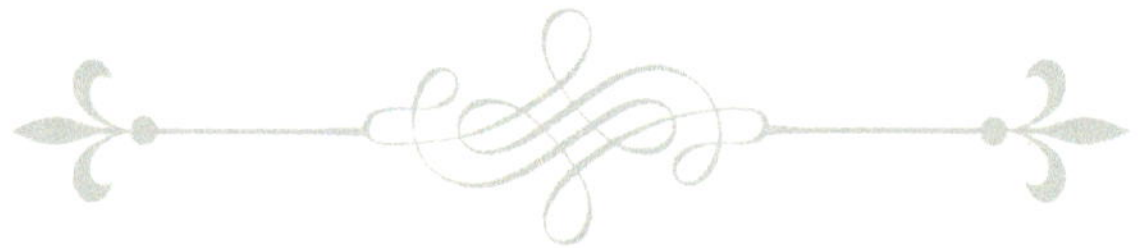

## Inspiring Shannon Estuary Sunrise

**S**unrises typically are more intense during Autumn and Spring, as the sun's angle accentuates the refractive nature of moisture and particles in the sky. This November sunrise over the Shannon Estuary is a perfect example. It's one of my all-time favourite sunrises, which is why I chose it for the cover of this book.

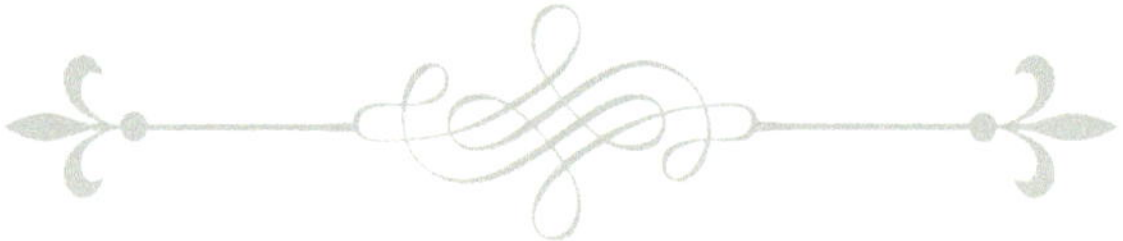

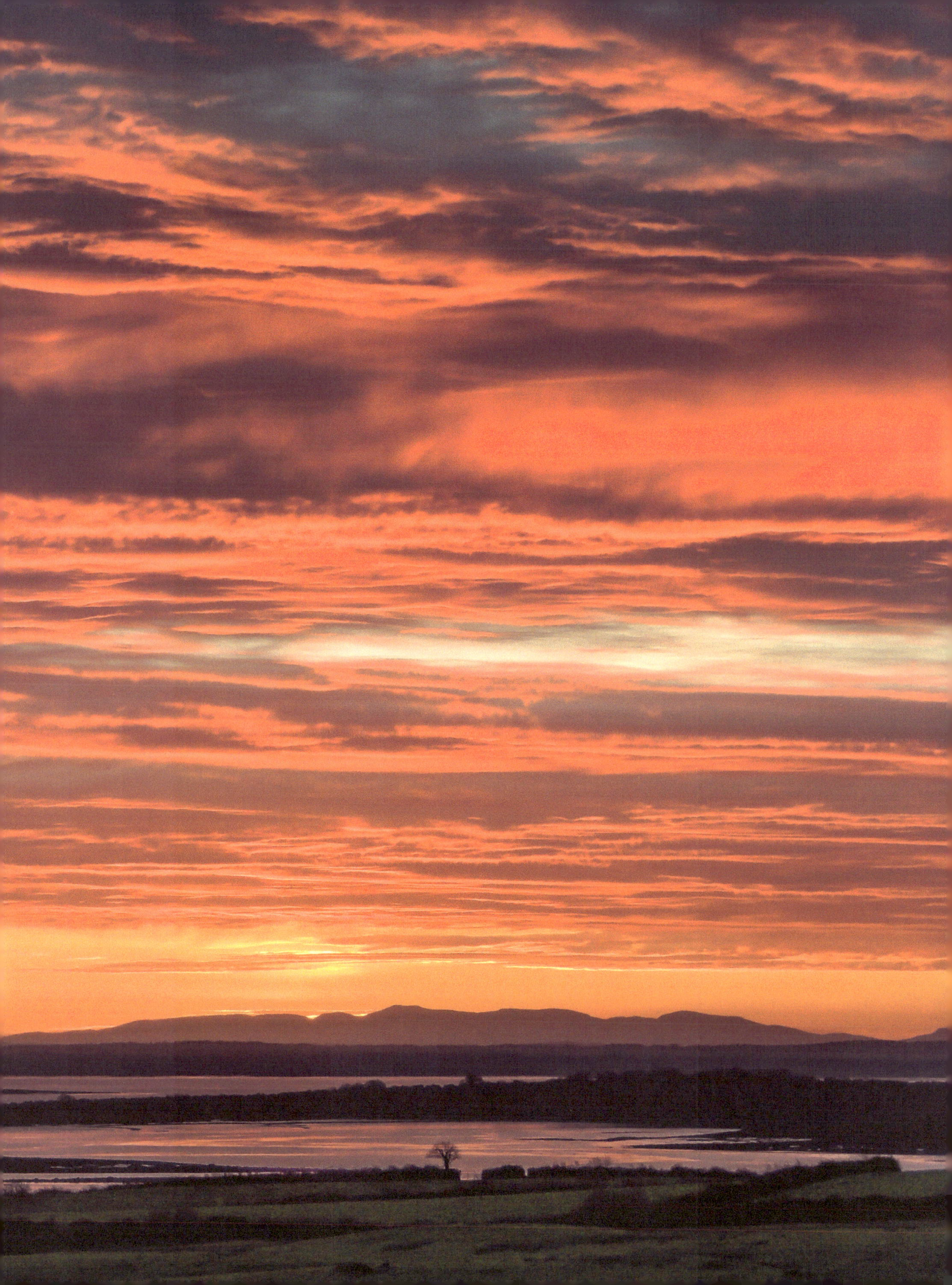

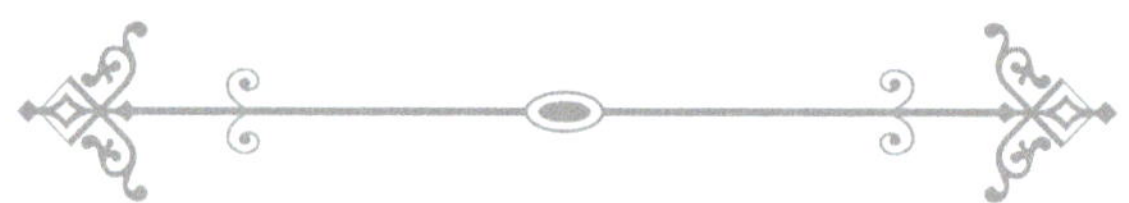

## Wall of Sun Pushes Westward

**A** wall of yellow light from this November sunrise pushes Westward over County Limerick toward the Shannon Estuary and the shores of County Clare.

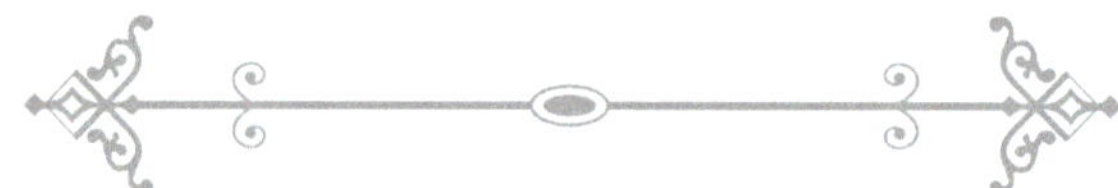

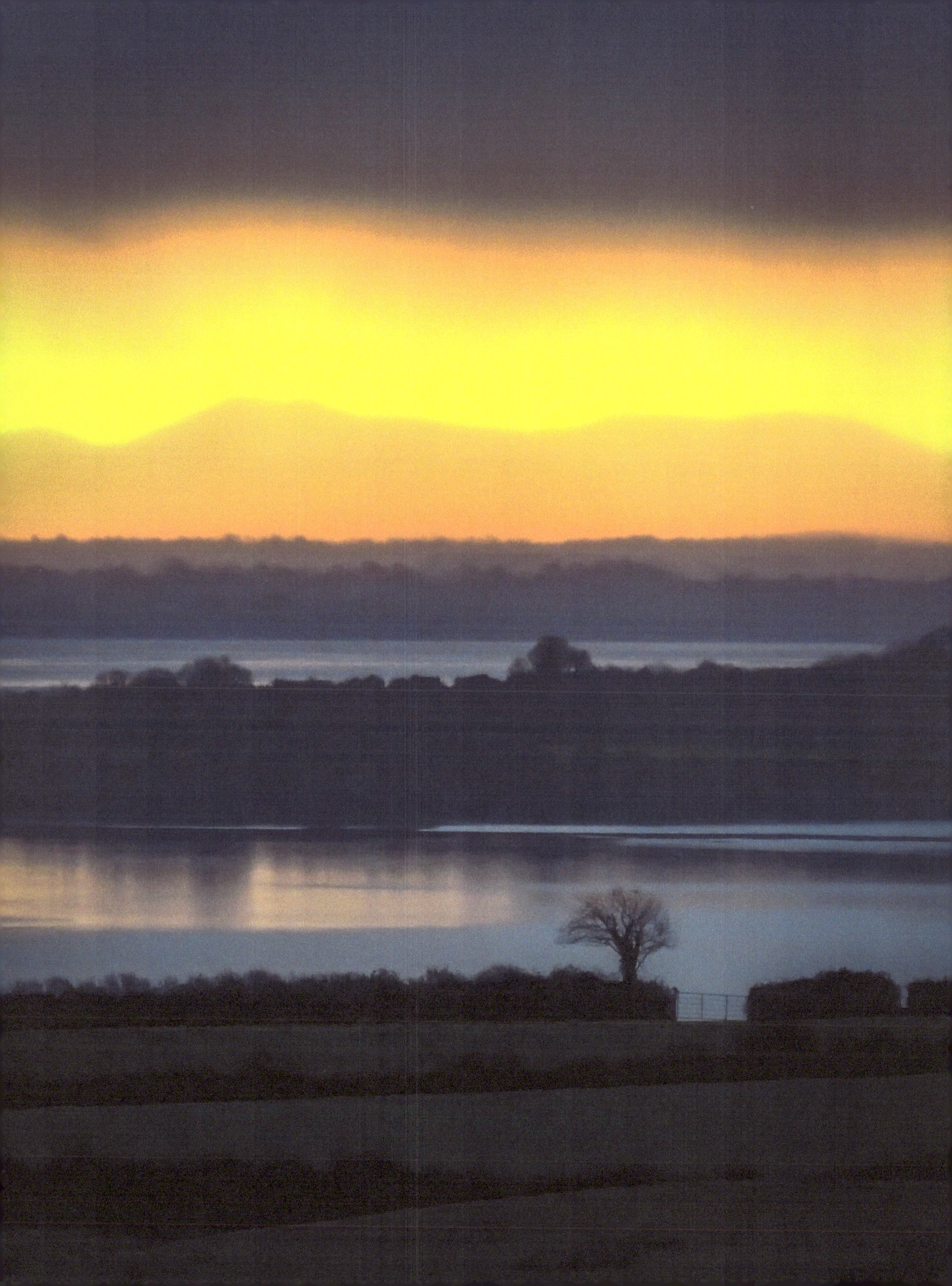

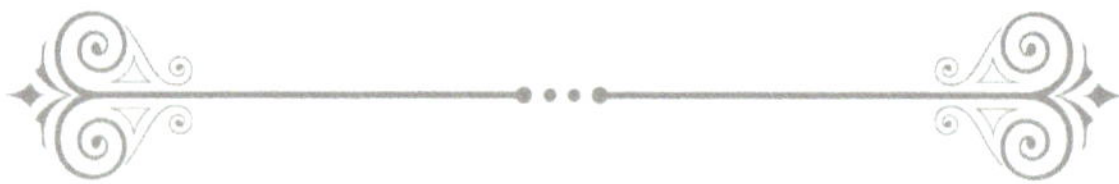

## Pastel Colours and Clouds of Cotton

Pastel colours behind clouds of cotton greet this soft Winter morning in December 2017 over Ireland's Shannon Estuary.

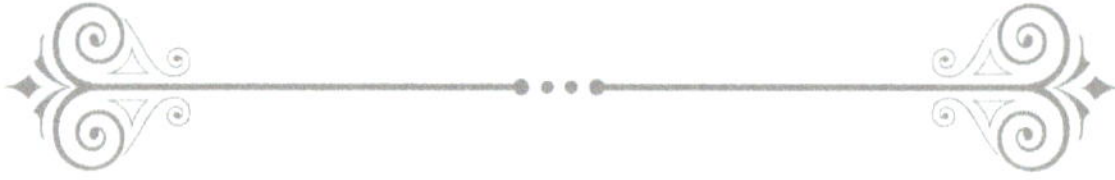

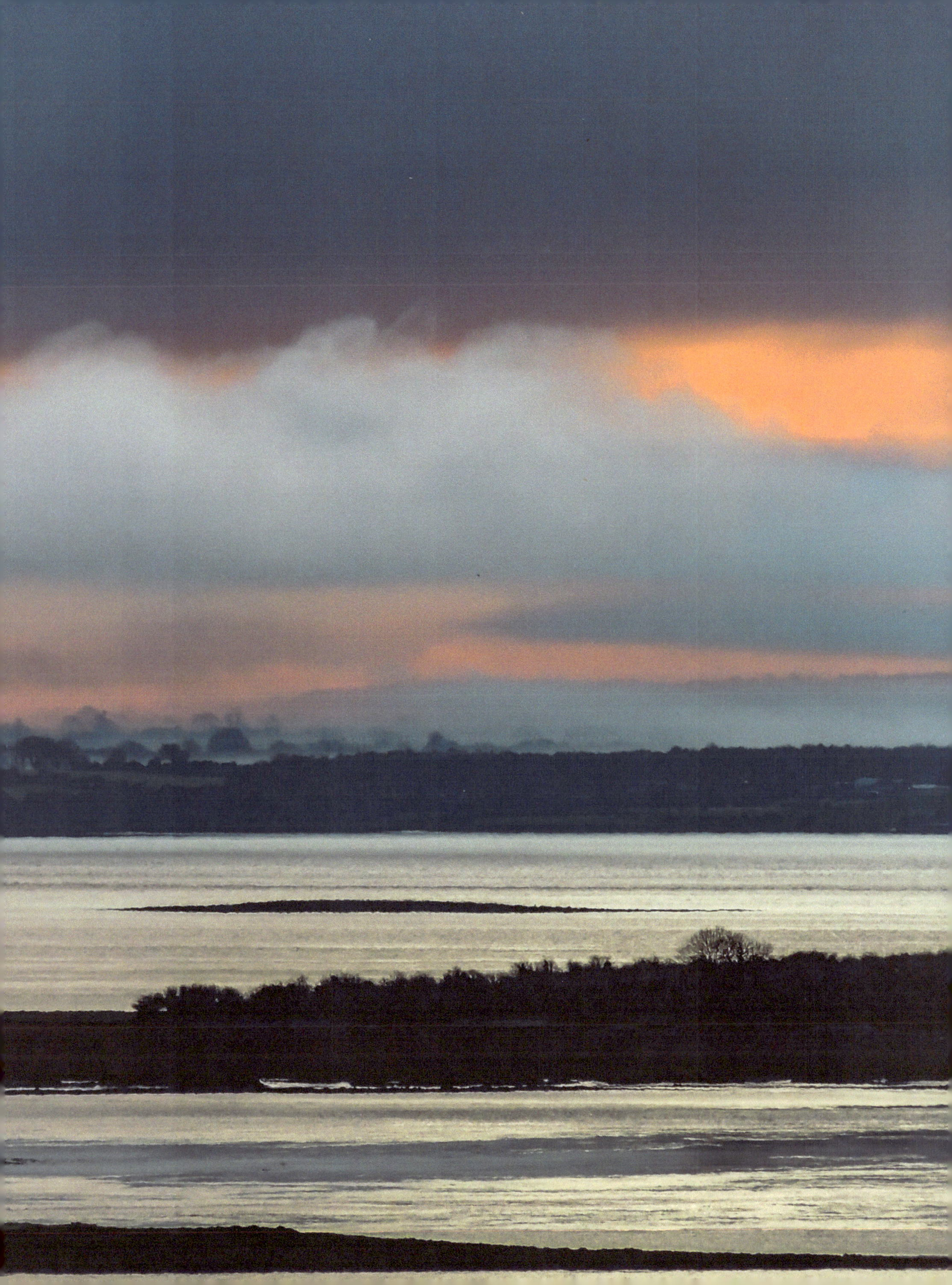

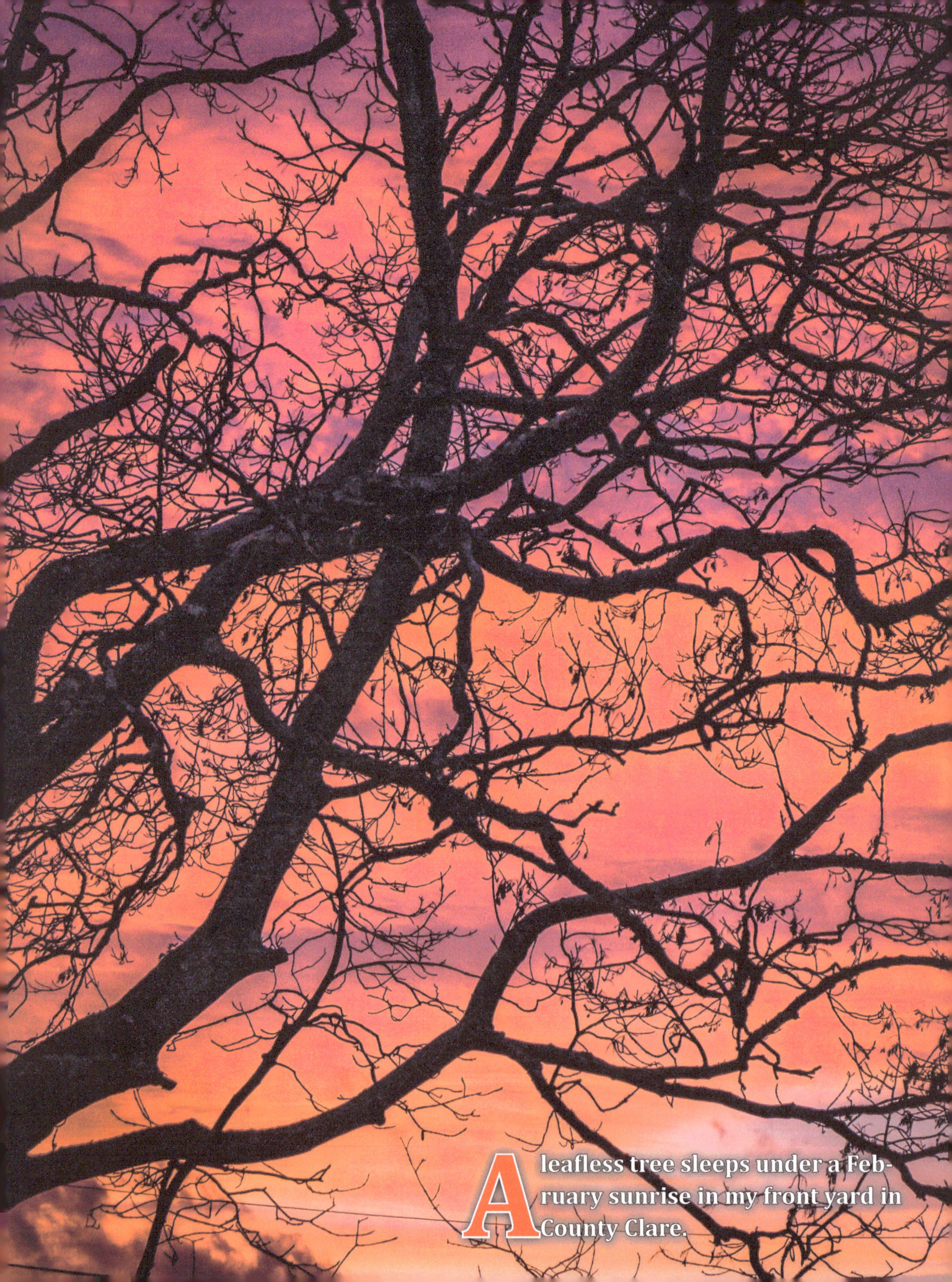

A leafless tree sleeps under a February sunrise in my front yard in County Clare.

# Acknowledgments

For me, this is the most important page in this book. It's where I get to express my gratitude to those who have played an important part in my universe during the creative process resulting in these pages. Many of the people listed here likely don't even realize their influence in this project.

Thank you!

**Vislan Alberto Truett Prado**

**Valeria Truett de la Cruz**

**Francis, Helen & Anthony Murphy**

**Maureen & John Ginnane**

**David & Elizabeth Odell**

**Rita Montgomery**

**Sue & Ted Downward**

**Bridget O'Sullivan**

**Charles & Marilyn Hansen**

**Chuck & Daiana Hansen**

**Michael & Christine Michael**

**Noel & Eimear O'Grady**

**Eddie & Yvonne Murphy**

**Dr. Finbar Fitzpatrick**

**Pauline McDermott-Smith,** *Ireland of a Thousand Welcomes*

**Roman Petrenko**

**Donna Winkhart Lab**

**Cheryl Phillips**

**Toni Parolisi**

**Tonia Bartlett**

**Marilyn Moloney**

**Maureen O'Dea**

# *More kind words from Fans...*

*"James' sunrises slowly open my soul to the blessings of another day. The force that runs through me when I view them speaks of the connection I have with my ancestors, my beliefs, MY IRELAND!"*
**~ Cindi O'Shea**

*"The sunrises James captures are beautiful and awe inspiring. They make me smile and feel good. Getting to Ireland would be awesome, but seeing his photographs gives me happy vibes and a warm heart."*
**~ Gretchen Hinkson**

*"James A. Truett really knows how to capture the rays of the sun and use them to inspire his fans' imagination... Open the book and let it take you to the land of beauty and imagination."* **~ Eileen Moore**

*"I may never get to Ireland, but James' beautiful pictures make my heart happy! Extraordinary work!"*
**~ Dawn Pofahl**

*"Your photos heal the soul. I pray all the time to be in Ireland one day. Your pictures keep my dream alive."* **~ Elizabeth George**

*"In James' photographs the wonderful, magical and colourful scenery of the Emerald Island of Ireland makes you travel there with your fantasy.  Thank you, my friend, for the nice work."* **~ Maria Rouvitsa**

*"Your photos of sunrises are absolutely gorgeous, it makes me wish I was there watching them. The scenery looks so quiet and peaceful, the colours are so beautiful. I could spend the rest of my life looking at scenery like that."* **~ Catherine Ryan**

*"My dream has always been to go to Ireland. The photographs that James takes are absolutely phenomenal. I have never seen colors the way he captures them. They are so vibrant they come to life."*
**~ Karen Peebles**

*"James Truett's Irish sunrises remind me of the magical days we spent there and call me home."*
**~ Jane Carlile Baker**

*"I look forward every morning to seeing your photo of the day. I love sunrises and sunsets and take lots of pictures. County Clare is very close to my heart, I have wonderful memories of Clare.I visit very dear friends in Ennis. The contrast of colors in your photos are so amazing. My home is Waterford which also has lovely scenery. Keep taking photos and writing which gives  pleasure to so many people."*
**~ Brigid Guarino**

*"Sunrise. Beautiful start to a new day!"* **~ Shirley Nail**

*"Your sunrises are a beautiful start to any day!! The colors make me smile! Thank you, James A. Truett."*
**~ Carole Guenther**

*"If a picture paints a thousand words then James Truett's sunrise photos speak volumes. If you've experienced a sunrise in Ireland these pictures will ignite your memories. If you've never seen one in person you will feel as though you have after viewing these. The photos capture the beauty and awe of a new day in County Clare  and provide the opportunity to reflect and renew one's spirit."*  **~ Irene Toto**

*"Having been to Ireland once, the magic of the countryside and people have never left my heart and mind. The images that James has managed to capture are simply amazing and bring back many pleasant memories. Until I can get back, James's book will have to do. Thank you for sharing your magical world with the rest of us across the big pond."* **~ Nancy Olson**

*"I have been to Ireland five times since 2009. The weather has been great most of the time and I got to enjoy sunrises and sunsets, The pictures that James puts in his books and posts on line bring back the beauty of County Clare that I so enjoy. Gran was born in Liscannor and installed the love of Clare in me."*
**~ Pam Javadian**

*"After living in Ireland for more than seven years and being back in Germany for nine  years, I am still homesick. So, looking at those amazing pictures I can imagine being there ('home') for a short while. James, you catch those wonderful sunrises I experienced myself. The light is so enchanting, isn't it? Very beautiful pictures which will take you to Ireland without having to travel."* **~ Birgit Lehmann**

*"My great-grandfather came to America from Coolmeen, a small village near Kildysart on the Shannon Estuary. I've made numerous trips 'home' to Ireland and relish photographs of one of the world's most beautiful countries. No Irish photographer compares with James Truett. No matter the site nor the subject, Mr. Truett captures the true essence of Irish beauty. Every time. His work is absolutely amazing."*
**~ Mike Spellecy**

*"Mr. Truett's photography is an excellent depiction of the raw beauty of County Clare sunrises and sunsets! Song: Every man has got the finest you ever see now, bar me now. Any day sure one o' them would say, she'll agree now you'll see now. At night they'd fight as to which o' them was right for the color of her eyes and hair. But not a word from me was ever heard about the darlin' girl  from Clare!"*
**~ Leila O'Shea**

*"When I look at all your photos it transports me to another time. My Grandfather came from Ireland and never knowing him, your photos keep my  heart in Ireland and history of generations before. Thank you for all your efforts to share light and love to those willing to accept and feel it."*
**~ Fatimah Abdullah**

*"Being from the Philippines, I was absolutely blown away by the beauty and majesty captured by James in his magnificent images of the beauty of County Clare. You have provided me with wonderful unforgettable memories of your amazing part of the world."* **~ Amalia Grace Dela Pena**

*"I love your photography, James. Indeed, you have captured the mystique and beauty of Ireland  with your "Sunrises of County Clare". Although I never witnessed an actual sunrise in County Clare, I can now close my eyes and view the warm reds fading to golds on an early  morning walk along a country road on the outskirts of Doolin  or Kilkee. The colors warm one's soul and mix with the cool morning breeze as I walk.  It is as if I am looking through the lens with you at the flaming red as the sun slowly emerges over the horizon and colors mix magically changing the landscape around them. It is truly a meditation on the beauty of Ireland."* **~ Joan Morrissey Kluck**

# Other Books by James A. Truett

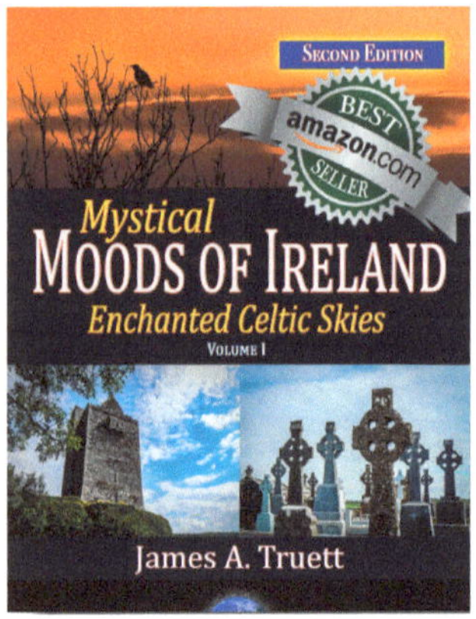

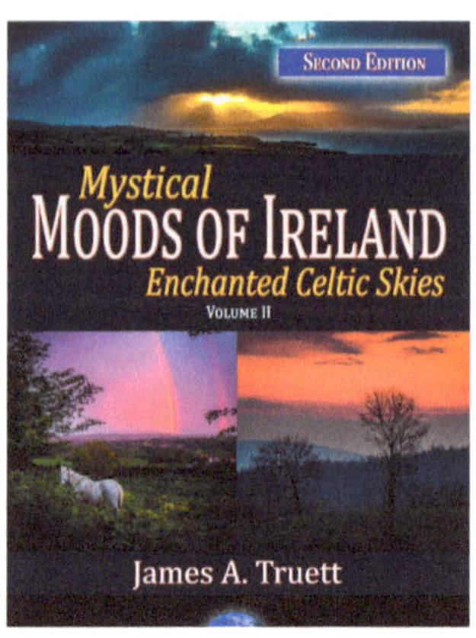

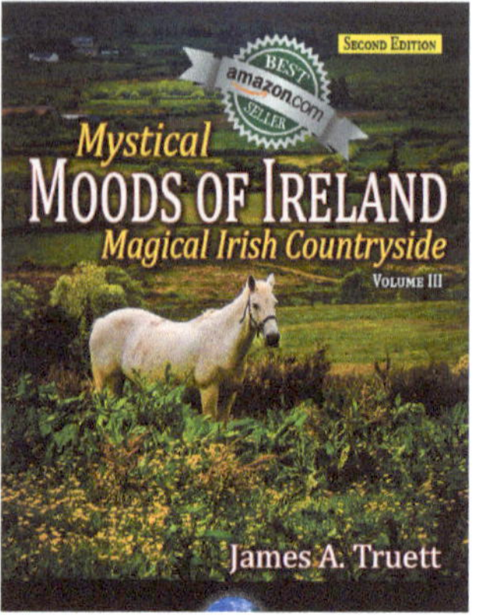

**Enchanted Celtic Skies, Book 1**
*Mystical Moods of Ireland, Vol. I*

**Enchanted Celtic Skies, Book 2**
*Mystical Moods of Ireland, Vol. II*

**Magical Irish Countryside**
*Mystical Moods of Ireland, Vol III*

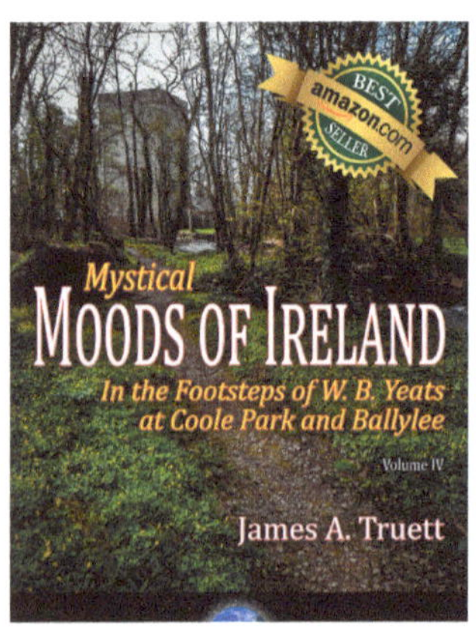

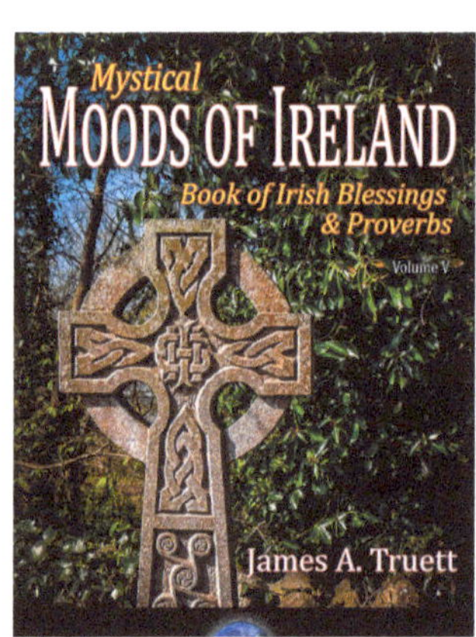

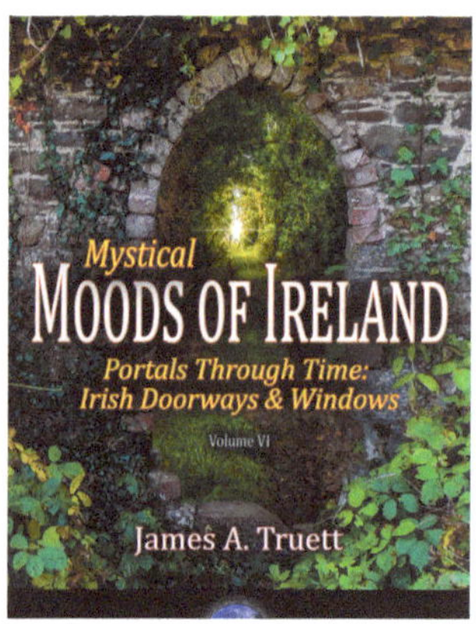

**In the Footsteps of W. B. Yeats
at Coole Park and Ballylee**
*Mystical Moods of Ireland, Vol IV*

**Book of Irish Blessings
& Proverbs**
*Mystical Moods of Ireland, Vol V*

**Portals Through Time: Irish
Doorways & Windows**
*Mystical Moods of Ireland, Vol VI*

*Available at all major booksellers and* MoodsofIreland.Com

*Follow James A. Truett's adventures,
and get free previews of his books here:*
www.JamesATruett.Com/subscribe

# About the Author

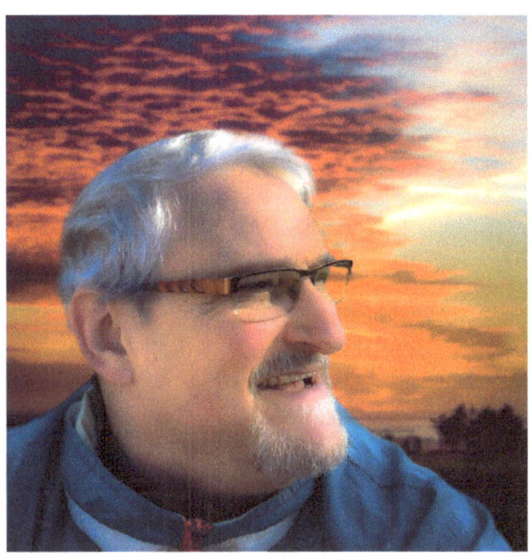

**J**ames A. Truett, author of the bestselling seven-book *Mystical Moods of Ireland* series of photo essays, is a former Associated Press journalist whose work has appeared in most major newspapers and many web sites around the world.

He has survived a shooting (his camera took the bullet!), a raging forest wildfire and Los Angeles traffic during his journeys as a sailor, private pilot and adventurer, travelling extensively throughout the United States, Canada, Mexico, Central America, Ireland and Scotland.

A second-generation Irish immigrant born in Alaska, he retraced the path of his grandmother and settled near the family farm in County Clare more than a decade ago, immersing himself in the inspiring and soul-stirring natural beauty of Ireland.

When not exploring the Irish countryside, he enjoys cooking and introducing his Irish family to international cuisine during family lunches. All have survived so far.

He battles his addiction to news by sharing his inspirational images and Irish blessings on his popular Facebook and Intagram pages.

***Connect with James A. Truett on Social Media:***
www.JamesATruett.Com/social

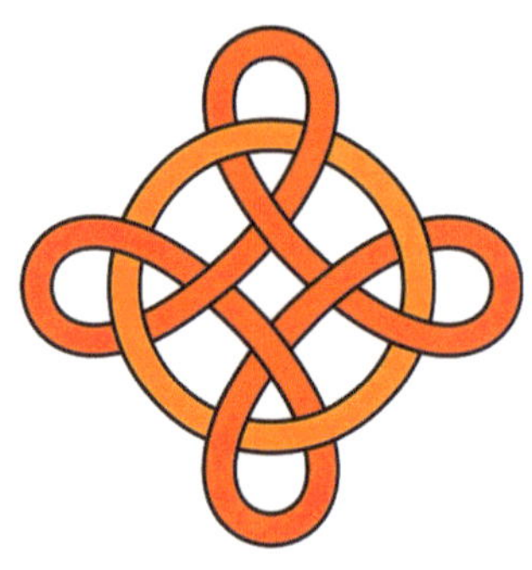

# Irish Blessing

*"May every sunrise
hold more promise,
And every sunset
hold more peace."*

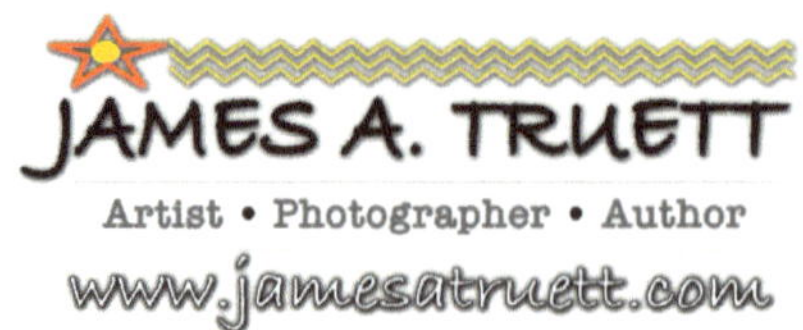